USING
COMMON
Initiation Services

A Practical Guide to the New Services

Gilly Myers

CHURCH HOUSE
PUBLISHING

PRAXIS

To Duncan, Caroline, Nicholas and Francis —
much loved companions on the pilgrimage, without
whose encouragement this book would not exist.

Church House Publishing
Church House
Great Smith Street
London SW1P 3NZ

ISBN   0 7151 2006 9

Published 2000 by Church House Publishing and *Praxis*

Copyright ©   *Praxis 2000*

Telephone   020 7898 1557
Fax   020 7898 1449
Email   *copyright@c-of-e.org.uk*

Printed by   The Cromwell Press Ltd, Trowbridge, Wiltshire

Typeset in   11pt Sabon and 11.5pt Gill Sans
               by Pioneer Associates (Graphic) Ltd, Perthshire

Contents

What is *Praxis*?

Praxis was formed in 1990, sponsored by the Liturgical Commission of the Church of England, the Alcuin Club, and the Group for the Renewal of Worship (GROW). It exists to provide and support liturgical education in the Church of England.

Its aims are:

- to enrich the practice and understanding of worship in the Church of England;

- to serve congregations and clergy in their exploration of the call to worship;

- to provide a forum in which different worshipping traditions can meet and interact.

The name *Praxis* comes from the Greek word for action. It emphasizes our practical concerns and conveys our conviction that worship is a primary expression of the Christian faith.

Praxis runs an annual programme of day conferences and residential workshops around the country, organized either centrally or by *Praxis* regions (informal networks of diocesan liturgical committees).

You can find out more about *Praxis* from our web site: www.sarum.ac.uk/praxis/

For a copy of the *Praxis* programme and details of how to affiliate, contact the *Praxis* office:

Praxis
St Matthew's House
20 Great Peter Street
LONDON
SW1P 2BU
Tel: 020 7222 3704
Fax: 020 7233 0255
Email: praxis@stmw.globalnet.co.uk

Foreword

Those who produced the *Common Worship* services wanted to provide liturgical resources that encourage worshipping communities to take account of the pastoral needs of the congregation and the mission imperative of worship that engages with the surrounding culture.

The synodical process has, rightly, focused on the texts, the structures and the rubrics. But the services will only come to life and reach their potential as living encounters with God in the nitty-gritty of worship in parish churches, hospitals and prison chapels, school halls and other centres of worship. *Praxis* was set up by the Liturgical Commission in partnership with The Group for the Renewal of Worship (GROW) and the Alcuin Club to foster just such a practical approach to liturgy – working at grass roots level to support real churches who are seeking to make their regular worship better. *Praxis* has been running training events and courses to this end for ten years and it is a great step forward to see the combination of deeper undersatanding and better practice coming together in print.

The *Using Common Worship* series is a creative partnership between *Praxis* and Church House Publishing which will help all of us to make the most of *Common Worship*. Each volume bridges the gap between the bare texts and the experience of using those texts in worship. Full of practical advice, backed up with the underlying thinking from members of the Liturgical Commission, these books will be a valuable tool to put alongside the *Common Worship* volumes on the shelves of every worship leader in the Church of England.

✠ *David Sarum*
Chairman of the Liturgical Commission

Acknowledgements

The publisher gratefully acknowledges permission to reproduce copyright material in this book. Every effort has been made to trace and contact copyright holders. If there are any inadvertent omissions we apologize to those concerned and undertake to include suitable acknowledgements in all future editions. Page numbers are indicated in parentheses.

Scripture quotations from the *Good News Bible* published by The Bible Societies/HarperCollins Publishers Ltd., UK, are copyright © American Bible Society, 1966, 1971, 1976, 1992.

Scripture quotations from the *New Revised Standard Version Bible: Anglicized Edition* are copyright © 1989, 1995, Division of Christian Education of the National Council of the Churches of Christ in the USA. Used by permission. All rights reserved.

Christian Computer Art: 'Make note' icon (p. 49, etc.) from the *Christian Clip Art* disk. Used by permission (www.CC-Art.com).

Faber and Faber Ltd: Extract from T. S. Eliot, *Four Quartets* (p. 1). Reproduced by permission of the publisher.

The General Synod of the Anglican Church of Canada: 'Those who are baptized are called to worship and serve God' (p. 33); Prayer over the Water (p. 117). Adapted from (or excerpted from) *The Book of Alternative Services of the Anglican Church of Canada* © The General Synod of the Anglican Church of Canada 1985. Used with permission.

The Joint Liturgical Group of Great Britain: Affirmation of Baptismal Faith (p. 18) from *The Daily Office Revised* © The Joint Liturgical Group of Great Britain. Used by permission.

The Rt Revd David Stancliffe: 'N., God has called you by name and made you his own' (p. 95). Used by permission.

Preface

Writing during Holy Week, I am reminded that Easter is, traditionally, the Church's greatest baptismal festival and of how the Church's patterns of baptism have changed over the centuries. Nowadays, in the Church of England, we do not hold all – or even most – of our baptisms on the day of Christ's resurrection. Yet whenever and wherever we baptize, we are reminded of our own baptism, our call to discipleship and the centrality of baptism to our mission.

It is essential to have the best tools for this mission and, just as crucially, to know how to use such implements to their best advantage. Over a number of years the Liturgical Commission and the General Synod have produced some tools for our use: the *Common Worship* Initiation Services. They have been carefully forged and it is now our responsibility to become skilled at using them and to apply them most aptly to each local church and congregation.

Since the Initiation Services were authorized in 1998, I have spent much time with clergy and lay people who are trying to interpret the *Common Worship* services and to use them most effectively in a variety of local situations. I have also spent time visiting churches of all traditions to see how they are using the *Common Worship* baptism service to welcome new Christians into their communities. Clergy and lay people have shared their thoughts, opinions and good ideas and I am sure that thinking will continue to be reshaped as churches grow used to a fresh approach to initiation.

Common Worship characteristically provides flexibility and variety within certain common frameworks; this in itself challenges us to prepare our worship in new ways. The Initiation Services, in particular, are very different to their predecessors, expressing the culmination of world-wide reassessment of the Church's baptismal practices. There is much to discover. It is my hope that this book will deepen our understanding of the nature of these 'tools' and stimulate the very best creative use of these resources as we seek both to worship God and to welcome new worshippers to follow in his Way.

Gilly Myers
Maundy Thursday 2000

Introduction
Jeremy Haselock

'In my beginning is my end', wrote T. S. Eliot in *Four Quartets*, and again:

> We shall not cease from exploration
> And the end of all our exploring
> Will be to arrive where we started
> And know the place for the first time.

Eliot might have been writing about an insight of the contemporary renewal of baptismal theology, for the Church has discovered or, perhaps more accurately, rediscovered that baptism is not only a beginning but a process and a goal in the Christian life. The baptism of Jesus, described so vividly in the gospels, marked the realization, in the midst of our history, of hopes long-desired and anticipated by the prophets: the presence of Emmanuel – God-with-us – and the inauguration of God's reign which destroys death and restores humanity to life.

As many great artists have shown us, the baptism of the Christ – the Anointed One (Acts 10.38) – made visible the life of the Trinity and revealed the coming kingdom of God. For Jesus himself, the experience in the waters of the Jordan represented not simply the beginning of his ministry but an outpouring of the Holy Spirit, consecrating him to God's way of salvation.

For the followers of Christ also, baptism is far more than a beginning; it is both the mark of God's ownership (cf. Ezekiel 9.4) and the sign of our calling. Rather like the name which runs all the way through the stick of rock our children buy and enjoy at the seaside, baptism is the seal which marks out who we are right to the end. It confirms our God-given identity, dignity and vocation and delineates the boundaries of the life to which we are called. The new *Common Worship* baptism service draws upon the enormous variety of imagery used in the New Testament to illustrate the richness of all that God gives us through the sacrament.

The exploration of all these images and all the implications of baptism which they open up is a vital part of the life of the Christian. Baptism is not something to undergo and then leave behind, but a sign to be entered into, a promise to be taken up, at every stage of the journey of faith. So, to those who are new to the Christian faith and are exploring it for the first time, God extends his invitation to set out on the path that leads to the font. To those who have been baptized in infancy, God offers the opportunity to reappropriate this sign at every stage of life, so that they may enter again and again into the identity and calling that baptism signifies. This is equally true for children growing up within the life of the Church; adolescents struggling to establish their own identity; and adults affirming their baptismal faith for the first time on their own behalf or beginning to investigate the claims of Christ from a background of no faith at all.

The initiation services in *Common Worship* – Baptism, Confirmation and Affirmation of Baptismal Faith – offer not just beginnings but ways of entering again into our baptism. These liturgies ought, with effective teaching, to lead to a popular reappraisal of the importance and centrality of the sacrament of baptism. For, seen in this way, baptism is very much more than a 'moment', a 'beginning', or a key to the door of the other sacraments. It is also, vitally, a 'process' or 'journey', truly both beginning and destination and the voyage of discovery in between.

All this may be new to most of us. Where did all these new ideas come from?

A bit of history

By far the majority of older members of the Church of England today have no recollection of their baptism. For most people it is an event which took place in infancy, usually in the context of a celebration for the immediate family and a few special friends.

Conscious of the actual performance of the rite or not, youngsters were nevertheless made aware of its significance and importance during their preparation for confirmation. As part one of a two-stage process, baptism was seen as an essential precondition for an episcopal laying-on of hands which, by bestowing the gift of the Holy Spirit, somehow completed the mysterious procedure of Christian initiation and incorporation into the mystical body of Christ 'which is the blessed company of all faithful people'. So, completed by confirmation, baptism was the key that opened the door to the other sacraments, particularly Holy Communion, and could be looked back to as the moment which marked the beginning of the Christian life.

Thirty years ago this two-stage view of Christian initiation could be supported by scholarly interpretation of the New Testament material, a particular view of the tradition of the Early Church and the prevailing understanding of the doctrine and practice lying behind the primary liturgical resource then available to the Church of England – the 1662 *Book of Common Prayer*. Today this is not possible. Simply stated, critical examination of the patristic evidence reveals, to put it bluntly, that the requirement that baptism should be completed by confirmation is based on an exaggerated view of the importance of what was originally simply a post-baptismal ceremony.

Recent developments

- After years of reflection on baptismal policy, the Church of England produced, amongst other things, the 'Ely Report' in 1971 and the 'Knaresborough Report' in 1985, both of which affirmed the central principle that 'sacramental initiation is complete in baptism' and opened up the debate on the admission of children to Holy Communion before confirmation.

- Anglican liturgists meeting in Toronto in 1991 for the fourth International Anglican Liturgical Consultation, engaged in an in-depth review of Christian initiation in contemporary Anglicanism and issued a ground-breaking statement, *Walk in Newness of Life*, which, amongst many other important matters, set confirmation in its proper relation to baptism with this firm recommendation:

> Baptism is complete sacramental initiation and leads to participation in the eucharist. Confirmation and other rites of affirmation have a continuing pastoral role in the renewal of faith among the baptized but are in no way to be seen as a completion of baptism or as necessary for admission to communion.

- The very explicit statement from Toronto set an agenda for serious reform of our Church of England liturgical materials. General Synod realized that, if taken seriously, this liturgical revision would also need to incorporate insights from the radical renewal of baptismal theology which had emerged ecumenically and been expressed in such statements as the 1982 World Council of Churches Faith and Order document *Baptism, Eucharist and Ministry* (often referred to as the Lima or BEM text) and which had informed the Toronto deliberations.

- In July 1991 Synod passed a motion which not only required the provision of new services but also a paper on patterns of nurture in the faith with particular regard to the catechumenate.

- The Liturgical Commission was already aware it would be asked to revise our initiation services – the end of the period of authorization for those in *The Alternative Service Book 1980* (hereafter ASB) was within sight. It welcomed the new climate for baptismal reform and the additional opportunity to participate in a study of the viability of a catechumenate model of Christian faith-exploration and nurture to inform the revision process.

- In partnership with members of the Board of Mission and the Board of Education, members of the Commission produced the report *On the Way* and presented it to Synod in 1995.

On the Way found its final form under the pen of the late and much missed Michael Vasey, himself a vital force in the Liturgical Commission that drafted the new rites. The report, like the Toronto deliberations before it, has been crucially influential in the shaping of the new services.

Some questions

So the process of revision undertaken by the Liturgical Commission, and, it must be said, the subsequent General Synod Revision Committee which played a significant role in drafting the services as finally approved, was informed and shaped by the events and debates outlined above. From the 1991 Toronto Statement four important issues emerged. The services in *Common Worship*, insofar as they differ from the provision in the ASB, reflect a deliberate liturgical response to these issues and their underlying theology. The four issues being addressed can perhaps be summarized best in question form:

- *What precisely is happening in baptism?* What are we doing when, in response to the Lord's command (Matthew 28.19b), we baptize in the name of the Father and of the Son and of the Holy Spirit? Does a sacrament which has for many years been understood and administered using a 'moment' model now need to be complemented by a new 'process' or 'journey' model if its true significance in the ongoing Christian life is to be appreciated and valued? A re-examination of the traditional biblical metaphors used in the baptismal liturgies, and the exploration of some less familiar ones employed for the first time in the new rite, will help our understanding of this issue.

- *Can the same basic liturgy be used for the baptism of both infants and those able to answer for themselves, i.e. for both inarticulate babies and young children and those who are older and have progressed through a catechumenate process?* This of course begs the question of whether we should be baptizing infants in any case. Consideration of the part to be played in the mission of the Church by the joyful celebration of an accessible, readily understood rite of initiation is vital to this question, particularly since Toronto stressed that new texts should not be separated from God's mission beyond the Church.

- *How can we make clear in our rites and ceremonies that although baptism is the beginning in the classic sense, it holds within itself all the other elements of the Christian life?* This is perhaps the most critical question of all if we are not to fall into the error of earlier generations and see baptism merely as the gateway to the other sacraments, but rather understand it authentically as the sign that effectively points Christians to their true identity, character and calling.

- *How best do we clarify the issue of admission to Holy Communion in relation to baptism and confirmation without diminishing the importance and significance of the latter?*

Some answers

What are we doing in Baptism?

Christians believe that by ritually plunging or immersing an individual in water and invoking the Holy Trinity over them we are claiming for that individual and the world in which we live God's achievement and promises, as shown forth and enacted in the life, death and resurrection of Jesus Christ. This process of claiming involves separation from 'this world', understood in the sense of all that is alienated from God, and reception into a universal community, the Church. This community is God-centred and has as one of its main aims and objectives the provision of an environment within which God's children can grow into the fullness of the pattern of Christ. Its mission is also to be God's agent for redeeming the world. Through baptism we are freed from sin and reborn as children of God; we become members of Christ and are incorporated into the Church and made sharers in her mission.

The 'world' in the New Testament sense, articulated most clearly in the first letter of John, is characterized by its failure in its vocation to 'give God glory' (Romans 1.21) and is thus subject to forces other than God. If we are prepared to use this language, the root remedy for this alienation can be described as the creation of relationship in a community centred on God and with a new pattern of life. To grow and develop rightly, new human beings need to be incorporated into this God-centred community from the start.

In the New Testament this separation from 'the world' and reception into a new set of relationships is expressed by a wonderful richness of complementary metaphors.

The Introduction to the basic Holy Baptism service introduces a number of these metaphors at the very outset of the rite (indicated here in bold type):

> Our Lord Jesus Christ has told us
> that to enter the kingdom of heaven
> we must be **born again** of water and the Spirit,
> and has given us baptism as the sign and seal of this
> **new birth**.
> Here we are **washed** by the Holy Spirit and **made clean**.
> Here we are **clothed** with Christ,
> **dying** to sin that we may **live his risen life**.
> As children of God, we have a new dignity
> and God calls us to fullness of life.

Most of these have inspired the traditional language of the baptismal liturgies of the mainstream Churches but others, as yet, have not really figured adequately. The use of hitherto less well-explored biblical metaphors in the renewed baptismal liturgy will, I believe, greatly widen our understanding of the sacrament. This will inevitably prove difficult for those whose understanding of baptism is wholly shaped by paschal images, but the effort is worthwhile. Because they figure in the new services, and particularly in the seasonal provision, I think it important to look at some of these metaphors, both the familiar and the less so.

Some rediscovered metaphors

Liberation This is clearly a familiar image because the Exodus experience, particularly the passage through the Red Sea, has been seen from earliest times as a type of baptism (1 Corinthians 10.1–4). Deliverance from the power of darkness (Colossians 1.13) and freedom from sin (Revelation 1.5b) are both included in this metaphor of separation.

After the Signing with the Cross the ideas of deliverance, restoration and exodus are powerfully conveyed in this prayer.

> May almighty God **deliver you** from the
>   powers of darkness,
> **restore in you** the image of his glory,
> and **lead you** in the light and obedience of Christ.

New creation This can only mean that reception into the Church which is the body of Christ is a radical making new (Galatians 6.15, 2 Corinthians 5.17). This is linked to new birth, as explained by Jesus to Nicodemus (John 3.3ff.) and mentioned in the letter of James (1.18).

The Prayer over the Water provided in the seasonal material for Epiphany/Baptism of Christ/Trinity contains this image:

> We bless you for **your new creation**,
> **brought to birth** by water and the Spirit

Illumination The opening of eyes, ears and hearts to the truth is an essential part of reception into the God-centred community (Ephesians 1.18, Hebrews 6.4). This is explored most fully in John, that most sacramentally-minded of gospels, in the story of the healing of the man born blind (John 9).

The Decision is introduced as follows:

> In baptism, God calls us **out of darkness into his marvellous light**.

Reconciliation Between humankind and God, and within the human race itself, all enmity is broken down and removed by the saving acts of Christ (Romans 5.10, 2 Corinthians 5.19).

Dying This is a particularly rich and familiar metaphor which must include drowning (and hence the paradox that baptism is 'life through drowning') and also burial (Romans 6.3f.). Christ himself uses the language of baptism to describe the ordeal of passion and death he has to undergo (Luke 12.50, Mark 10.38). The obvious balancing image is that of resurrection into newness of life (Romans 6.4ff. and Colossians 2.12; 3.1ff.)

The Easter/Pentecost seasonal Introduction is particularly rich in these metaphors:

> God raised Jesus Christ from the dead
> and sent the Holy Spirit to recall the whole world to himself.
> In baptism **we die to sin** and **rise to newness of
>   life in Christ**.
> Here we find **rebirth** in the Spirit,
> and set our minds on his heavenly gifts.
> As children of God, we are continually **created anew**,
> as we walk the path of faith,
> and feed on the forgiveness of his healing grace.

Stripping By this is meant putting off the old nature (Colossians 3.9) and the Christian analogue to circumcision (Colossians 2.11). This idea of separation is balanced by the reception image of clothing – putting on Christ as if putting on a garment (Galatians 3.27) and putting on the new nature (Colossians 3.10).

> *If the newly baptized are clothed with a white robe . . . a minister
> may say*
>
> You have been clothed with Christ.
> As many as are baptized into Christ have put on Christ.

Recognition This involves receiving the name of Christ (James 2.7) and being called by name by God (cf. Isaiah 43.1).

Building The activity of incorporating men and women as living stones into a new community, a temple not made with hands (1 Corinthians 3.9ff., Ephesians 2.19–21, 1 Peter 2.4f.).

See, for example, the seasonal Collect provided for Easter/Pentecost:

> Father of our Lord Jesus Christ,
> from whose wounded side flowed life for the world:
> raise your people from sin and death
> and **build them as living stones
> into the spiritual temple of your Church**;
> through Jesus Christ . . .

In all these metaphors it is the action of God which comes first, just as repentance – metanoia – is classically seen not as a human achievement but as a response to God's loving initiative.

The baptismal journey

God's action is not just imaged in moments or events but also with journey motifs. The Exodus theme is particularly rich in this respect, which is perhaps why it has been the controlling image in our baptismal liturgy for so long. Just as the escape from Egypt and the liberation at the Red Sea lead on to Sinai, the sealing of a new covenant and the gift of Torah, so Easter leads on to Pentecost when, with the gift of the Holy Spirit, God's law is written on the heart as promised by Jeremiah (Jeremiah 31.31-4). The Church is the new Israel of God, a people on pilgrimage to the Promised Land, marching through the desert of temptation and testing but with guidance and special provision for the journey (1 Corinthians 10.1-13). These people on the march are spiritually armed and ready to be Christ's willing soldiers and servants (Ephesians 6.10-18, 2 Timothy 2.3-5, 15).

Separation from the 'world' and reception into the new community are important in themselves but they also inaugurate the 'journey' or 'process'. Baptismal reception into the believing community is the beginning of a voyage of discovery. It is the beginning of a pilgrimage of growth into the pattern of Christ, in which obedience is learned through testing and temptation, just as the baptism of Christ was followed by a period of absorption and testing (Mark 1.12 and parallels, Hebrews 5.8-9).

The life of Jesus was lived out, as it were, between two baptisms: the baptism he received at the hands of John at the very place where the chosen people first entered into the Promised Land (Mark 1.9), and the baptism of his death (Mark 10.38), the Pasch, when he passed from this world to his Father, from death to life. In the same way our life is lived between two baptisms. Our whole life is an exodus in which we are tried and tested, but also fed and sustained. We travel with our passports stamped, as it were, with the character of our first water baptism (the Red Sea experience), which carries within it the promise of our second baptism (Jordan) when we pass through death to life in the kingdom. Jesus is our pioneer in this journey, as the hymn-writer Charles Wesley so memorably phrased it:

> Jesu, be thou our constant guide;
> Then, when the word is given,
> Bid Jordan's narrow stream divide,
> And bring us safe to heaven.

An accompanied journey

The voyage of Christian discovery will pass through different stages of maturity and responsibility; there will be the inevitable crises, times when the wind blows us off-course, becalmings, reversals and renewals, which it may be appropriate for the community to acknowledge liturgically and thereby show support in a public way. Baptism is the sacrament of faith. But individual faith needs the community of belief that is the Church and only within that community can each of the faithful believe. The Christian voyage is a voyage undertaken in convoy with others. Although every person's journey is unique, it cannot be made alone. The learner on the way has three immense resources to call upon, three wells from which to draw strength, knowledge and understanding. The first is Jesus the fellow traveller (Luke 24.13-35). The second is the Church, the community of those who follow the way. The third is the Bible, which contains all that is necessary to lead us to salvation through faith in Jesus Christ (2 Timothy 3.15). Faith is indeed required for baptism, but it need not be a perfect and mature faith; rather, it may be a beginning which is called to develop.

The divine purpose in forming the community and bringing it to maturity in the stature of Christ (Ephesians 4.13) is to use it to establish the kingdom and to bring the world to perfection. This is the mission of the Church. These goals are set both in this world, where there is a social agenda and responsibility for bringing about a new world order, and in the world to come, with individual responsibility for entry into the kingdom. The Holy Spirit, poured out in the sacraments of initiation, is the foretaste and pledge of that world to come (Romans 8.23, 2 Corinthians 1.22, Hebrews 6.5). The process of becoming partakers of the divine nature (2 Peter 1.4) begins at baptism.

Of the Fathers, Irenaeus expressed this concept of divinization most memorably when he wrote of the second person of the Trinity, 'he became man that we might become God'. Baptism can thus be seen as the beginning which holds within itself its destination, as already revealed but not yet worked out. This perception illuminates the way in which 'moment' includes within itself 'process' and points beyond the here and now in which we live to the eternal for which we are sealed. The concept of divinization also enables us to see how reception into the new community is also reception into the very life of God-in-Trinity, for we are putting on Christ who in his baptism was acknowledged as Son by the Father and indwelt by the Spirit.

A single rite for both infants and those who can answer for themselves

Even if we continue to believe in infant baptism, where the evidence of the sheer gratuitousness of the grace of salvation is particularly clear, we must nevertheless face up to the fact that adult initiation will become increasingly important and frequent in the life of the Church. Fewer and fewer infants are automatically brought to baptism for reasons of folk religion and more and more young people and adults are coming to faith through outreach and such Christian basics courses as *Alpha*, *Emmaus* and *Credo*. Because it is vital that baptism received in infancy is not at some stage later in life regarded as ineffective or of less significance than adult baptism, it is essential that the same rite is used for both, with little or no change in the texts or ceremonies save where this is obviously required by the circumstances.

In order to achieve this single rite, the Commission has sought to make God's prevenient grace central to the whole action (Romans 5.6-8). With both adult and infant baptism it is the action of God which comes first. Baptism is a grace and gift of God that does not presuppose any human merit.

The president addresses the whole congregation thus

Faith is the gift of God to his people.
In baptism the Lord is adding to our number those whom
    he is calling.

Parents, sponsors and adult candidates themselves all respond to God's gracious and loving initiative. In the case of infants the response is made vicariously, by the godparents within the Church's fellowship of faith, and with the expectation that in due time the children will take on the responsibilities of the Christian life for themselves. In the case of mature persons, the candidates' profession of faith precedes the moment of baptism and this profession of faith should be understood as having been drawn from them by the prevenient grace of God.

The one rite of baptism should be seen as acted evangelism. It proclaims the victory of God in Christ's death and resurrection, light out of the darkness of sin and a new creation out of the old world of chaos. It establishes the Church as Christ's body and marks out the individual believers as those called to participate in the work of the kingdom. In recognizing those whom God has called and bringing them into his community, it also inspires those who are already part of that community to renew their commitment to the mission of the Church.

Thus, underlying the new rite is the theme of covenant to show clearly that baptism is the visible sign and ritual celebration of incorporation into the people of the New Covenant, sealed by Christ's death. The covenant is given by God (Exodus 19.3-6, 2 Corinthians 3.6) to infants or adults and the obligations it carries with it unfold gradually. These are the response to the grace of God which the Spirit makes possible as the individual matures and accepts responsibility.

In revising the rite the Commission has tried to emphasize the social aspect of baptism alongside and prior to the merely individual. The baptismal sign points forward and back not just for the individual but for the community also. Through active participation in the liturgy, the assembled congregation is brought to re-focus on its dignity as God's holy and priestly people and prompted to renew its understanding of why it has come together. Increased involvement on the part of the assembly in, for example, presenting and supporting the candidates, possibly hearing their testimonies and joining with them in affirming the faith of the Church, heightens the sense that the baptism of individuals is a significant event for the whole Church.

> *The president addresses the whole congregation*
>
> Faith is the gift of God to his people.
> In baptism the Lord is **adding to our number** those
>   whom he is calling.
> People of God, will you **welcome** *these children/candidates*
>   and **uphold** *them* in *their* new life in Christ?
> *All* **With the help of God, we will.**

The texts make clear the nature of the new community and new world into which the candidates are being initiated. Strengthening the affirmations and renunciations in the service sharpens the difference between the old world the candidate is leaving and the new where the Church is already located.

For most of us in the Church of England the most remarkable difference between the old and new baptismal liturgies will be the provision of rites which stress the catechumenal process by marking the stages on the way and giving the community the opportunity to appropriate them. These new rites are currently in preparation but there is a strong indication of the way in which things are moving in the work-in-progress document, *Rites on the Way* (GS Misc 530). The initiation services already available really need to be seen in the wider context of *Rites on the Way* in order to understand how revised and renewed sacramental practice is to be fully integrated with people's lifelong journey of faith.

Since the authorization of the *Rite of Christian Initiation of Adults*, the catechumenate has been a common route for adult candidates in the Roman Catholic Church. *Ad Gentes*, Vatican II's document on the missionary activity of the Church, had long ago made it clear that the process of Christian initiation

> should not be left entirely to the priests and catechists, but should be the concern of the whole Christian community, especially of the sponsors, so that from the beginning the catechumens will feel that they belong to the people of God.

Learning from this, the Church of England needs, by bringing about a real change of culture, to extend the idea of continuing post-baptismal teaching, nurture and formation both to the families of infants brought to baptism and to the community into which they are baptized. Courses currently available, such as *Alpha*, *Emmaus* and *Credo*, are of immense use in this respect. The Church's responsibility in baptism demands that its practice is clearly associated with a commitment to subsequent Christian nurture. Growth in faith and participation in the life of the Church are integral to baptism and not additions to it. Infant baptism is open to real objection if this ongoing nurturing process is not clearly signalled in the liturgy.

Baptism is the source from which the entire Christian life springs

Growth and mission, the seeds of which are sown in baptism, both require catechesis – induction into the whole of Christian living: worship, prayer, doctrine, ethics, witness, service. As the Toronto Statement puts it:

> The journey into faith involves a process that includes awareness of God, recognition of God's work in Christ, entering into the Christian story through the scriptures, turning to Christ as Lord, incorporation into the body of Christ, nurture within the worshipping community, and being equipped and commissioned for ministry and mission within God's world.

Where the newly baptized are unable to answer for themselves, a minister addresses the congregation, parents and godparents, using these or similar words . . .

As [*these children*] grow up, *they* will need the help and encouragement of the Christian community, so that *they* may learn to know God in public worship and private prayer, follow Jesus Christ in the life of faith, serve *their* neighbour after the example of Christ, and in due course come to confirmation.

In the Reformation pattern we have inherited from the sixteenth century, this has normally been expressed by baptism being followed by confirmation, together with preparation for holy communion and ministry as part of the royal priesthood. In recent years other patterns have emerged in many provinces of the Anglican Communion, in the Roman Catholic Church and in some of the Churches of the Reformation, and, with them, an acceptance of a measure of diversity. Whatever the pattern followed, the equipping of God's people for ministry requires continuing education for all. This catechesis and continuing education must aim at bringing about the ongoing discovery of what was done in baptism and the giving of new identity. It must lead to the continual renewal of putting on Christ and taking up the cross which teaches Christians to see weakness, suffering and failure as the locus of redemption, glory and victory, and to welcome new stages on the journey as the unfolding of God's baptismal covenant and promise.

As the baptismal life with all its implications is lived out, it will be seen that sacramentally and therefore liturgically it involves far more than the Reformation pattern of baptism, confirmation and holy communion. Baptism is not simply a sign of individual and corporate forgiveness and renewal, it points to the way in which God in Christ is overthrowing an order of life infected with sin and death and bringing to birth a renewed creation which is alive with the healing presence of the Holy Spirit. Baptism is surely a sign of God's decisive act of identification with human beings in their weakness and a promise of his commitment to human well-being in every area of life.

The Commission intends to provide what might be called liturgies of baptismal life which will include: reconciliation in the case of straying or falling into sin; healing if inhibited by sickness; deliverance if enslaved by habit or addiction; and maybe even preparation for death – the completion of the baptismal journey. These rites will be opportunities for individuals and communities to reappropriate the grace of baptism and direct their feet once more upon the baptismal journey. The implication for the continuing process of liturgical creativity is that the new rites for all the different pastoral offices should, by their shape, structure and content, help to unfold what was begun in baptism.

Baptism, Confirmation and Admission to Holy Communion

It is important to recognize two conflicting views on the

relationship between baptism and confirmation. On the one hand, the tradition of the Eastern and Western Church and the discipline of the Church of England hold that confirmation is an integral part of the initiation process. In the Church of England confirmation is always administered by the bishop and is the normal precondition for receiving holy communion.

On the other hand, however, it has been argued that baptism is the complete sacramental initiation and leads directly into participation in the Eucharist. On this principle, confirmation is seen as a rite of affirmation but not the completion of baptism and is relegated to the status of a desirable, but not essential or necessary, pastoral rite. It is difficult to reconcile these views, even though both enshrine important insights, particularly as our bishops still see the administration of confirmation very much as their primary sacramental contact with their flock and are in consequence anxious not to allow the status of the rite to be diminished or to permit it to be devolved to presbyters.

The view that baptism is complete Christian initiation might seem not only to depreciate confirmation but also to deny to a certain extent the process element in the sacramental event which we examined earlier. Initiation into the sphere of the Spirit, which is indeed complete in baptism, must be distinguished from the appropriation of the gifts of the Spirit, which can take place at different stages and occasions. As we have seen, it is proper to speak both of moment and process in relation to Christian initiation and it may be that we have to come to terms with the possibility of some sort of 'extended' confirmation. The 'liturgies of baptismal life' mentioned earlier will present a number of repeatable ways of appropriating baptismal grace, as the Christian life progresses and develops.

The rite of baptism in the 1662 *Book of Common Prayer* makes it clear that the entire profession of the Christian life is represented in the action of baptism. After all, dying and rising again with Christ is the pattern upon which we lead a virtuous and godly life, and baptism provides a model for the way in which we should view our continual need to repent of sin and be restored, to grow and increase day by day in the Holy Spirit. Confirmation, according to the same 1662 provision, provides the opportunity for the candidates to renew the solemn promise made in their name at baptism, 'ratifying and confirming the same in their own persons'. It is the opportunity to appropriate personally that which was fully bestowed at baptism. The logic of the process model of initiation argues that such opportunities should be provided at other stages in Christian life and growth.

Affirmation of Baptismal Faith

Hence, in the new services, the rite of Affirmation of Baptismal Faith is provided for those who have lapsed from the faith and seek restoration and, more importantly, for those who are conscious of a fresh work of God in their lives and therefore wish to commit themselves publicly to God once again. After the pattern of confirmation – the same laying-on of hands but a different form of words – this rite provides just such a repeatable opportunity.

AFFIRMATION OF BAPTISMAL FAITH

The president **extends his/her hands** *towards those who seek to affirm their baptismal faith and says*

God of mercy and love,
in baptism you welcome the sinner
and restore the dead to life.
You create a clean heart in those who repent,
and give your Holy Spirit to those who ask.
Grant that these your servants may grow
into the fullness of the stature of Christ.
Equip them with the gifts of your Holy Spirit,
and fill them with faith in Jesus Christ
and with love for all your people,
in the service of your kingdom. **Amen.**

The president **lays his/her hand on** *each one, saying*

N, may God renew his life within you
that you may confess his name this day and for ever.
Amen.

The resulting shape of the new baptism service

The theological framework which emerges from the consideration of what we are doing in baptism undergirds and shapes the new baptism service. In summary this framework can be expressed simply:

- **Separation** from the world of life alienated from God.

- **Reception** into a universal, God-centred community – the Church.

- **Transformation** of the individual and invitation to grow in grace and participate in the divine nature.

- **Mission** to work in co-operation with God in his work of redemption.

These four key themes stand as signs in the flow of the service to direct it on its way.

The service opens with God's welcome to the newcomer clearly understood: it is his prevenient grace that has brought the candidate to the font in the first place. The vital role of the community in welcoming and nurturing the new Christian is also made clear at the outset of the service. The assembly receives the new Christian with joy and promises to uphold him or her on the journey of faith.

Separation from a world alienated from God is made clear by the strong wording of the Decision section and it would be sad to see these carefully crafted declarations abandoned in favour of the shorter versions by those for whom brevity is the controlling liturgical principle. The candidate opts for God and firmly renounces evil and the pomps of the devil. This section culminates in the **reception** of the sign of the cross, the clear signal that from now on the candidate wishes to be associated with Christ and his body, the Church.

The real substance of the **transformation** theme is to be found in the Prayers over the Water in their seasonal variety. The Holy Spirit is invoked over the baptismal water and asked to perform his work of transformation. This is reinforced by the post-baptismal prayer for the anointing of the Spirit who daily renews his own that they may grow in grace.

The **mission** of the newly baptized within the community of the faithful and to the world is made clear in a number of ways. They are reminded that all the baptized are called to worship and serve God and invited to 'proclaim by word and example the good news of God in Christ'. Newly incorporated into a holy people, a royal priesthood, the new Christians may be encouraged to exercise their ministry for the first time in leading the Prayers of Intercession, the Prayer of the Faithful.

The importance of *missio* or sending out is strengthened by the transfer to the end of the service of the now very popular tradition of giving a lighted candle to the newly baptized. This then becomes not only a rite of illumination but also a call to mission: 'Shine as a light in the world to the glory of God the Father.'

In conclusion

One of the earliest names for the Christian faith is 'the way'. Those who have embarked on the process of Christian initiation can truly be said to be 'on the way'. The goal of this journey is relationship with God the Holy Trinity, life and worship in the Church, and service and witness in the world. The route is a way of discipleship: learning to worship with the Church, growing in prayer, listening to the Scriptures and serving our neighbour.

The new *Common Worship* liturgy of baptism reflects these new insights, as must the rites we have yet to devise to mark the stages of the initiation process. Responding to the challenge of taking them seriously will change the perspective of both priests and people. 'Christian initiation', as Michael Vasey wrote so memorably in his summary of the recommendations of the *On the Way* report, 'is not about socialising people into the rules and practice of a club. It involves encounter with the dynamic presence and mission of the living God.'

▌The People of God

In this chapter... we shall explore how the different parts of the baptized community each play their own part in the service of Holy Baptism. We shall begin with the congregation, move on to the candidates, and then look at the roles of the 'special supporters' – the parents, godparents and sponsors.

Who are we?

We all go through life collecting certificates and badges. No sooner have we been born than our parents have to register our existence and claim a birth certificate. As we grow, we gain certificates to prove that we have learnt to play a musical instrument to a particular standard, managed to swim a certain number of lengths in a swimming pool, or passed a number of examinations in a variety of subjects with grades that are for better or worse.

If we marry, we sign registers and are given a certificate at the marriage service. We may gain qualifications relating to our work, and so on. Certificates don't end there, either – for in death, certificates are produced on our behalf to show for certain that we are no longer around.

Badges are usually different. We wear them to show that we are members of something, or that we feel strongly for a cause to which we lend our support. From school crests on blazers and sweatshirts to ribbons and chains, badges say something about who we are and with whom we belong.

At baptism we are also given a certificate. We never know when we might need to use it, but it is attractive to look at and we can put it away with all the other important documents we keep.

Herein lies the problem. For centuries we, as members of the Church, have consigned our baptisms to an event in the past, filing away any significance together with the certificate we were given on that day. We look back and say that we *were* baptized, remembering the event (if we were old enough at the time) or recalling the stories we have been told about it, as we flick through the fading photographs.

Baptism itself, however, is more like a badge than a certificate, and this is what the Church has been rediscovering as it finds that living out our baptism is every bit as important as the fact that we were baptized in the first place. The badge we wear announces to all who see it that we belong to Christ and to his Church, and that we have certain characteristics common to the baptized community of faith. It is not only that we have *been* baptized, but also that we *are* baptized. Baptism shapes us and goes on shaping us, as we grow in our discipleship and live out our calling to be followers of Jesus Christ.

Who are we? We are the baptized community of Jesus' followers. We are the body of Christ, called to live and grow in him.

Baptism is not a spectator sport

Once we have recognized the lasting significance of baptism, then we shall begin to realize that we all have a continuing part to play – not only in living out our own baptism, but in preparing and nurturing those who come for baptism themselves.

We have seen lay ministry developing in leaps and bounds over the past few decades and, thankfully, it is no longer normal for the clergy to be the only people in a parish involved in baptism preparation and post-baptismal development. All sorts of people have a part to play, whether accompanying adult enquirers as they explore the faith, or preparing parents and godparents of infants who are brought to be baptized.

As a community of believers, however, we are all involved in baptism, and the *Common Worship* Initiation Services help each one of us to see our part, as we shall discover in the rest of this chapter.

The congregation

In the *Common Worship* service there are a number of points at which the congregation's part in baptism is revealed:

- Presentation

- Profession of Faith

- Welcome and Peace

- Commission

Presentation

'Are you going to do your bit?'

This is a paraphrase of one of the first questions asked in the baptism service. It's not addressed to the candidates, nor to the parents and godparents. It is addressed to the congregation!

> People of God, will you welcome *these children/candidates* and uphold *them* in *their* new life in Christ?
>
> *Presentation*

It is a clear recognition of the fact that the continuing support and encouragement of these candidates is our responsibility, shared with others. We are called to accompany one another as we travel the Way, and not to abandon new believers to their own resources the minute the service ends.

This, of course, makes absolutely no sense at all if none of the regular congregation are actually present at the service – and Canon B 21 makes it clear that they should be, anyway. This is nothing new. What the question does underline, however, is the fact that the congregation has to be there in order to demonstrate the existence and nature of the baptized community into which the candidate is being initiated.

> every minister ... shall normally administer the sacrament of Holy Baptism on Sundays at public worship when the most number of people come together.
>
> *from Canon B 21*

23

Profession of Faith

In the ASB baptism, the candidates (or parents and godparents) were asked to affirm their faith in the trinitarian God, on their own in a short question and answer form.

In *Common Worship*, everybody makes the Profession of Faith together. The whole congregation joins in.

Brothers and sisters, I ask you to profess
together with *these candidates*
the faith of the Church.

Profession of Faith

Another difference is that the Apostles' Creed is normally used rather than the shorter affirmation of faith. The creed is divided into three parts, each prefaced by a question leading naturally into the response. The president asks if we believe in the Father, Son and Spirit in turn, and we reply with the appropriate words:

Do you believe and trust in God the Father?
All **I believe in God, the Father almighty,
creator of heaven and earth.**

Do you believe and trust in his Son Jesus Christ?
All **I believe in Jesus Christ, his only Son, our Lord,
who was conceived by the Holy Spirit,
born of the Virgin Mary...**

Do you believe and trust in the Holy Spirit?
All **I believe in the Holy Spirit,
the holy catholic Church,
the communion of saints...**

Profession of Faith

After all, this is our *common* faith, and by joining in unison at this point, we act out the community into which the candidate is about to be baptized. We have already required the candidates to make their own personal declaration to follow Christ; that was their 'separation' stage mentioned in the Introduction. Their 'reception' into the household of God is now beginning; now we assure them that this is a faith we share. This is not a journey on which they have to embark alone.

Welcome and Peace

At this point the congregation has the opportunity to enfold the candidates into the fellowship of faith by saying the Welcome and sharing the Peace. If there is time to exchange a sign of peace, then we can make a more personal connection with the candidates and their families, to demonstrate the reality of what we have said, albeit briefly at this point.

Commission

The Commission is a new feature of the Initiation Services, and there are two different options to choose between, depending on the age of the candidate. Whichever is used, the Commission comes immediately after the baptism.

When infants are baptized, the Commission is addressed partly to the congregation and partly to the parents and godparents. In case members of the congregation are still complacent about their responsibilities towards a newly baptized infant, mistakenly thinking that the continued nurture in the faith will be left solely in the hands of parents and godparents, they are reminded once again of the part they have to play.

As *these children* grow up, *they* will need the help and encouragement of the Christian community, so that *they* may learn to know God in public worship and private prayer, follow Jesus Christ in the life of faith, serve *their* neighbour after the example of Christ, and in due course come to confirmation.

Commission

When the Initiation Services were first authorized, the adult Commission was optional, whereas the infant Commission was not. Since then the rubrics have been amended. The infant

Commission need not be read word for word from the text, as long as the gist of it is included – either paraphrased at this point or included in the sermon.

The challenge we face

If the congregation is attentive at the Presentation and Commission, then it may well start to ask itself: 'What exactly does this mean, in practical terms?' This gives us an ideal opportunity to explore the question further as a Church.

In the *Common Worship* Initiation Services we cannot avoid the congregational responsibilities. We have seen that the Church throughout the world has grown in its understanding of baptism over the past few decades. We have come to appreciate the value and importance of increased involvement of the whole Christian assembly. For many theologians, liturgists and church leaders these concepts are no longer novel and are taken for granted. Yet for the vast majority of our regular congregations the implications will begin to dawn on them only through repeated use of the new services. Even then, it could well take a long time to sink in, and we may need to give a helping hand in assisting the church to come to grips with the theology implicit in the *Common Worship* provision.

In an ideal situation, where baptized adults continue to meet with the church fellowship, or where baptized children are brought regularly by parents or godparents, we should be able to fulfil what is expected of us. Child or adult, relationships with them will develop and they can be integrated into the church. As the children grow, they will be able to attend whatever groups and facilities are available to them and learn to express their faith and love of Jesus in a way appropriate to their age.

But what of those families who bring their child for baptism but never darken the doors of the church again? How can we do our bit, if they aren't prepared to do theirs? This is a serious question for many churches which are striving to maintain their integrity while, at the same time, wishing to extend the gracious and loving welcome characteristic of the God whom we worship. This struggle is not new. It has not arrived with the revised baptism services. What has happened, though, is that the

Common Worship services express our responsibilities more explicitly. If we know that we are unlikely to be able to carry them out, then we may begin to feel uncomfortable.

This is an ideal time to discuss our baptism policy as a church. Much of the uneasiness is rooted in a gulf between our own expectations and those of the candidates and their families. Perhaps we need to develop a completely fresh approach to baptism preparation, for example. The questions raised by the new services can be seen as an opportunity to explore these issues.

The candidates

As we look at the part of the candidates in the baptism service, let us investigate further the following ways of understanding baptism:

- Baptism as journey

- Baptism as story

- Baptism into the Way

Baptism as journey

A few years ago, Bishop John Finney published some revealing research into patterns of conversion to the Christian faith. He discovered that 69 per cent of Christians said that coming to faith had been a gradual process, rather than a sudden conversion. The average time for a gradual journey such as this was four years, and many Christians still considered themselves to be in a continual process of change.

Even people who have experienced a sudden conversion in their lives find themselves on an ongoing journey, as they discover more about God from day to day and learn how to follow him.

This element of process or journey is woven into the *Common Worship* Initiation Services. We talk about the candidates 'walking' – walking in the way of Christ, walking by the light of faith or walking in newness of life. We pray for them as they join the 'company of Christ's pilgrim people'. This is an accompanied journey, one on which the candidates are joined by the community of faith, at all their different stages and ages.

> In baptism God invites you on a life-long journey.
> Together with all God's people
> you must explore the way of Jesus . . .
>
> *Commission*

'Staged rites'

Some people find it helpful to use special prayers or services at various significant milestones along the path they tread as they enquire into the Christian faith, before they even reach the point of thinking about baptism. The first of these, for example, might be the moment when they realize that they really do want to take Christ seriously and find out more about him by joining an enquirers' course; another is the moment at which they know for certain that baptism is the path they want to take and they embark on serious preparation for the great event.

A collection of resources, under the working title *Rites on the Way*, is currently being prepared by the Liturgical Commission and aims to provide prayers and services for a whole range of significant occasions surrounding baptism.

As well as *Rites on the Way*, appropriate prayers and services can also be found in Thanksgiving for the Gift of a Child (in the *Common Worship* main volume and *Pastoral Services*); *Emmaus – The Way of Faith* (National Society/CHP and the Bible Society, 1996); *The Book of Occasional Services (USA)* (The Church Hymnal Corporation, New York, 1979); and *Rite of Christian Initiation of Adults* (the Roman Catholic staged initiation rites for adults; Geoffrey Chapman, London, 1987).

Prayers and services such as these, which recognize that a change in our lives is more often a series of steps rather than a sudden great leap, are described as 'staged rites'. *Common Worship* provides us with staged rites appropriate to other life-changing events, too, such as death and marriage. Here are just some of the prayers and services that might reflect the 'staged' nature of initiation:

Adults

- Welcoming of an 'enquirer' by a congregation.

- Prayers for an enquirers' group.

- Prayers to accompany significant Christian texts (the Apostles' Creed or Jesus' summary of the Law, for example) which could be presented to the enquirers, or studied by the enquirers' group at a certain point.

Parents of infant candidates

- Prayers to be used with the parents before or after the birth of the child – perhaps at home or in a hospital.

- Prayers before the baptism – perhaps in the preparation group, at home with the family or at the rehearsal in church.

- Prayers to be used with children and young people at certain points as they grow in their knowledge and love of Christ. They could also be presented with significant Christian texts – either in the congregation or in their children's/young people's groups.

This wealth of provision is not to constrain us into particular patterns. None of it is compulsory, but it may offer us more possibilities and ideas. These sorts of prayers can often be used by lay people; they can be used in ones or twos, in small or large groups and in congregations, depending on the circumstances.

Using such prayers or short forms of service to register these milestones in public worship is another way of involving the congregation in the whole of baptism; it can also be very affirming to the enquirers themselves. There is much to be explored in how to help people, young and old, to mark significant points along the way.

The Decision

This is the point in the baptism service when the candidate takes his or her next big step on the path to baptism. It represents a major turning point of his or her life.

The questions at the Decision are more complex than those in the ASB; they have more substance and are more demanding. Instead of three questions, there are now six and the candidates make it clear that they are well and truly turning their backs on all that is of the devil, evil, and sinful before declaring that they are turning, submitting and coming to Christ. At this point, the climax of their period of spiritual preparation for baptism, the candidates are marked with the sign of the cross. They are at the threshold of a whole new phase of their pilgrimage.

At this point in some ancient church traditions the candidates, who had started out facing west, would swivel right round to face the opposite direction as a symbol of their turning from darkness to light. The east, of course, is the direction from which the earth's light, the sun, dawns and in a sense this is the direction from which our daylight comes. This turning action would be immediately followed by the affirmation of faith.

Where there is a strong pastoral reason, the ASB questions at the Decision may be used instead of the *Common Worship* questions. For example, some candidates – for various reasons – might find the simplicity of the alternative questions easier to understand.

Baptism as story

One of the enormous privileges of being a Christian minister is hearing the most remarkable stories. People who consider themselves perfectly ordinary have the most amazing tales to tell. Some recall their searching for a path and a light in the darkness, some speak of encounters with God and miracles in their lives. Others give testimony to God's faithfulness and love through times of suffering and despair. Everyone, from the most tentative of enquirers to the most experienced of preachers, has a story to tell.

Testimony

Accounts of God's work in the people around us are a tremendous encouragement to us all, and in some churches it has long been the custom to ask people to come out to the front from time to time to share something of their story. In the *Common Worship* Initiation Services we now have an official opportunity to hear some of those testimonies! If any or all of the candidates, or the families of the candidate if it is a child, wish to say something, then they can have the opportunity at the Presentation.

A testimony does not have to be a life history; in fact it is usually better if it is not, unless time is of no concern whatsoever.

Standing up to speak in front of a congregation can be a daunting ordeal, and it needs to be stressed that this is not a compulsory requirement! However, if the candidates are willing to stand up to say something, then it is helpful to them if they are prepared for the experience. Here are some ideas:

- Suggest that they write out what they want to say and practise it at home.

- If the candidates are more confident, they can probably manage with bullet points.

- Anyone who thinks that they don't need notes at all should be advised to write out a very clear and concise plan in advance, as unstructured free-flow can get carried away!

- If there is someone who could interview them in the service then that is often easier than a candidate standing alone, giving a monologue. If the candidate dries up, then the other person can take over for a moment and redirect the conversation.

- Sometimes time is of the essence, or there are too many candidates to fit in, or they would be overcome with embarrassment at the thought of speaking in front of all those people (let alone in front of a bishop at confirmation!). In these cases, a special leaflet could be prepared in advance, full of written testimonies from any of the candidates who wished to contribute. They wouldn't have to be essays, and most people can put together 50–100 words about 'why I am here today'. Alternatively, this could be incorporated into the order of service.

If testimonies are going to be spoken, however, it would probably help everyone if there is a 'testimony rehearsal' before the event – not just for the sake of confidence but also to learn how to project one's voice or use a microphone.

Baptism into the Way

We have discovered that to think of baptism just as a beginning can be misleading, because we leave beginnings behind and move on to other things. Baptism is both a beginning *and* a way of life, and both these ways of looking at it are reflected in the *Common Worship* baptism service. Baptism is new birth and new life; it is also a continuing walk, by the light of faith, in the risen life of Jesus.

We are baptized into the mission of God and into ministry to his Church and world. These are such important aspects of our calling that the *Common Worship* Initiation Services have built upon previous baptismal liturgy, in the following ways:

- Commission

- Giving a lighted candle

Commission

The adult Commission (see facing page) immediately follows the baptism or confirmation, though it is optional. It is an excellent summary of the Christian life and pattern of discipleship, and is well worth using if the circumstances allow.

Having affirmed their calling to 'continue in the apostles' teaching and fellowship . . . in the *prayers*', and to offer '*prayer for the world and its leaders*', it might be fitting on occasion, if the individuals are sufficiently confident, for the newly baptized members of the church to follow the Commission by leading the intercessions, if they are included in the service.

Those who are baptized are called to worship and
serve God.

Will you continue in the apostles' teaching and fellowship,
in the breaking of bread, and in the prayers?
With the help of God, I will.

Will you persevere in resisting evil ... ?
With the help of God, I will.

Will you proclaim ...
the good news of God in Christ?
With the help of God, I will.

Will you seek and serve Christ in all people ... ?
With the help of God, I will.

Will you acknowledge Christ's authority over human
society ... ?
With the help of God, I will.

Adult Commission

Giving a lighted candle

Jesus said to his disciples, 'As the Father has sent me, so I send
you' (John 20.21). Followers of Jesus today continue to be sent
out in mission, to do their part in the work of God and the
building of God's kingdom. Jesus also told his disciples that they
were light to the world, and that no-one lights a lamp and then
hides it away; instead, they put it on a lampstand so that it can
light up the whole house (Matthew 5.14,15).

The medieval practice of giving a lighted candle to new disciples
after baptism is not in *The Book of Common Prayer*; it was
reintroduced in the series of services preceding the ASB. In this
now popular feature we send the candidates out of the church
building, echoing the words of Jesus:

> *All* **Shine as a light in the world**
> **to the glory of God the Father.**
>
> *Giving of a Lighted Candle*

In *Common Worship* the normal position for giving the candle has been moved to the end of the service, instead of straight after the baptism. In this context, just before the dismissal of the whole congregation, the command to shine out in the world beyond the church building makes much more sense and does not lose its impact in the way that it did in the ASB, when the candidates did not go out to 'shine as a light' at that point, but remained where they were for quite a while. And it was always odd that when such a powerful symbol was given in the middle of the service, it had to be extinguished a moment later because the candidate couldn't be left holding a dripping candle while the service continued for another half an hour.

Whichever way the minister or ministers leave the service at the end, we can include the candidates (and families, if the candidate is a child) and their flickering lights in our departure – sweeping them up into the procession or accompanying them out ourselves.

The 'special' supporters

Parents and godparents

There have been hours of debate, both in General Synod committees and beyond, over the necessary conditions of faith on the part of parents who bring their children for baptism. The debate will continue and this is not the place to air the arguments.

Needless to say, parents have the lion's share when it comes to influencing their children in matters of belief and lifestyle. They are left in no doubt as to their awesome responsibilities:

Parents and godparents . . .

Will you pray for [*these children*],
draw *them* by your example into the community of faith
and walk with *them* in the way of Christ? . . .

Will you care for *them*,
and help *them* to take their place
within the life and worship of Christ's Church?

Questions at the Presentation

As *their* parents and godparents, you have the prime
responsibility for guiding and helping [*these children*] in *their*
early years.

Commission

The church community pledges to support the parents in their
demanding task and prays for them to have the grace of God in
guiding their children into the way of faith.

What about parental faith?

The questions at the Decision, in the case of infant baptism, are
addressed 'through [the candidates'] parents, godparents and
sponsors'. They no longer have to answer 'for themselves' as in
the ASB, so this is a move back to the BCP tradition, where
parents and godparents answered 'in the name of this child'.

The question of whether parental faith should be a prerequisite to
the baptism of a child is a sensitive area, and there has been
much debate over it as the Initiation Services have made their
way through the synodical process. Jeremy Haselock refers to the
issue in his Introduction to this book, when he explains how the
Common Worship baptism rite works for both adults and
children. Two points are made very clearly in the *Common
Worship* service:

- Baptism is a gift from God, as is faith. God's prevenient grace
  and the stirring of the Holy Spirit draw our human response.
  God has made the first move.

- Anyone who is baptized, is baptized into the family of the Church, into the Christian community. This is the context of the continuing nurture of every Christian believer, as we worship, pray and study the Scriptures together, take our place in the fellowship of the body and draw inspiration and encouragement to serve and witness to God in the world.

When we baptize infants and children, we know that the ideal is for one or both of the parents to have faith themselves. We can then be sure that the child will be brought along to church and will grow up within the Christian community. The child will also have all the benefits of growing up in a home where the expression of Christian values is normal. Hopefully the parent(s) will pray with the child from the very beginning, delight in reading Bible stories from an early age, and wrestle honestly with all those tricky theological questions that children can come up with. All this will make sense of the baptism service, and we shall all be better able to keep the promises we make.

Clearly parental faith is very important, practically. But can it be *demanded*, theologically? The view (after much discussion) of both the Liturgical Commission and the General Synod Revision Committee was 'no'. For some in the Church of England this will raise acute questions about the very basis for infant baptism. In most of our Church of England parishes a majority of parents requesting infant baptism are not practising Christians. People often know which is their church even if they never go there, or if they go along just occasionally – at Christmas, perhaps, for the carol service. And they come along for baptism knowing exactly what they want from the Church and never thinking for a moment that we might have a different agenda.

At this point we are faced again, as we were earlier in the chapter, with an important challenge. How can we baptize and use the service with integrity? When parents so obviously have a completely different set of expectations from those of the church community, we clearly need to think carefully about appropriate and adequate preparation. We need to discuss and plan a realistic and effective baptism policy.

But at the end of the day, when we have spent time with the parents, explored their journey with them and tried to make connections with the road of faith, and explained the gospel in accessible and relevant ways, we may still see no outward sign of faith emerging. Nevertheless, when the parent continues to ask for the child's baptism, we cannot deny the sacrament. This is when the two points made above become especially important.

- We have to leave the matter in the hands of God. We cannot insist on a profession of faith from a parent before we will baptize the child. By God's grace the child has been brought, and we pray for God's grace in the life of the child.

- The church family has promised, with the help of God, to do whatever they can to uphold the child in its new life of faith. This is still our task and, if the parents don't bring the child to the church, then the church will have to consider how best to keep in touch.

Preparation and follow-up strategies for families of children brought to baptism are no small matter; they need prayerful consideration by PCCs and the commitment of the whole church family.

Sponsors

Some years ago, whilst working as a University Chaplain's Assistant, I had the joy of spending time with a number of people who, having left home for the first time, were asking for themselves the significant questions about life, the universe and everything. As the academic terms went by and some of them reached the point of baptism or confirmation, it was absolutely natural for those of us who had walked the path of enquiry with these individuals to stand alongside them at initiation. I was given the role of sponsor. I wasn't a godparent in the traditional sense of being responsible for the Christian upbringing of a child, but I was pledging myself, by the acceptance of the role, to hold these friends in my prayers, and encourage them in their discipleship in the future.

This is just one example of being a sponsor – it is flexible in definition and, although it is a new provision as far as the Initiation Services go, it is a role that has been recognized in the Canons of the Church of England for quite some time.

> When one who is of riper years is to be baptised he/she shall choose three, or at least two, to be his/her sponsors...
>
> *Canon B 23*

It is possible for a child to have sponsors in addition to godparents, but that would make sense only if there were some good reason for making a distinction between the two categories.

How many godparents and sponsors, and do they need to be baptized?

Full details about godparents and sponsors can be found in Canon B 23, but here is a summary.

- Each child should usually have at least three godparents, at least two of whom should be the same sex as the child, and at least one of whom should be of the opposite sex.

- If three godparents cannot be found, then one of each sex will suffice.

- Parents can be godparents to their own children as long as the child has at least one other godparent.

- Candidates who are 'of riper years' may choose their own sponsors – usually three but at least two.

- Godparents and sponsors are required to be baptized and (usually) confirmed.

In summary, baptism belongs to the whole people of God, old and young, ordained and lay. Some individuals will have a specific role and responsibility at particular baptisms, but everyone has a part to play. The whole church can pray, support and encourage each newly baptized Christian as he or she grows deeper into the faith and knowledge of our Lord Jesus Christ.

2 Symbols

In this chapter... we shall be looking into the symbols to be found in the *Common Worship* baptism service, and exploring how to use them to their best effect.

Every culture, community and religion in the world has its symbols. It is a natural human characteristic to identify and use symbols in life to give us a sense of meaning and identity.

A whole multitude of associations

Symbols are words, actions or pictures that lead us beyond themselves. They resonate within us, setting off a whole multitude of connections and associations. Sometimes symbols can be ambiguous and evoke contrasting responses in different individuals. Nevertheless, they are an intrinsic part of our humanity, and good symbols can have a remarkably positive effect.

> As when light hits a prism at exactly the right spot, colours are refracted and dispersed in so many directions, so is our thought refracted through the prismatic effects of an aptly chosen image.
>
> Stephen Platten, 'The Bible, symbolism and liturgy'[1]

Some symbols are universal, used the world over. Light, for instance, is a fundamental symbol of life and pregnant with meaning. Some symbols are more regional, like a single red rose, tenderly handed to a lover or tossed on to a coffin at a burial; some are cleverly contrived by serious marketing, like the Coca Cola logo; some are shallow and passing; others are known only to ourselves.

We have always had cultural symbols in this country, but it is worth noting an apparent increase in the desire to use symbols in our society today (think of the response to the death of Diana, Princess of Wales, for instance). As a culture we are moving away from valuing only the scientific and cerebral; we live in a decreasingly book-centred and word-centred culture and we often replace words with images and sounds and actions.

Symbols can have an astonishingly powerful effect on us, drawing us into deeper levels of our being, putting us in touch with feelings and meanings that are beyond words and verbal expression. They move and transport us into a different reality; they confront us with transcendence and God; and the most effective symbols take us far beyond our capacity to express exactly what is going on – that is their value and wonder. We can try to describe the effect of a particular symbol, but if we can contain it within a description then it is probably not a very good one.

Good symbols help us to worship: to express that which is profound and beyond words to God, who is also beyond our ability to express verbally and greater than we can ever imagine. The Holy Spirit works through these symbols, drawing us deeper into the presence of God.

Symbols and the Church of England

At the Reformation, a reaction against an unhelpful medieval multiplicity of symbolic ornamentation in worship resulted in the shunning of all but a few, and this is a legacy which continues to have a strong influence in many of our congregations. This is not the end of the matter, however, because in many other churches, right across the traditions and in many different forms of worship – healing services, funerals, marriages, all-age events – we have been rediscovering the value of symbolism and not been afraid to take a step on to what had long been considered forbidden territory.

This renewal of symbol and ritual has emerged in different forms in different parishes. In some it is performed with stylized order and precision, whilst in others it is more *ad hoc* and informal. It has evolved in the way that suits the local church. But however symbols are used, we often find that people are full of appreciation and eager for more.

The Liturgical Commission, acknowledging the power and helpfulness of good symbols in worship, has therefore encouraged the use of apt and appropriate symbols in worship. *Common Worship* in general has not been afraid to introduce new symbolism into the Church of England services, nor to enhance the place of the more familiar symbols.

These are the symbols found in the baptism services:

- water

- sign of the cross

- light (candles)

- oil

- clothing

Water

Water is *the* symbol of baptism and all others are secondary. It is the means by which we are washed or cleansed; in these waters we drown and die to our old life before being raised with Christ; these are the waters of birth as we are brought forth from the womb into new life; these are the waters through which we pass from the slavery of sin to freedom in Christ.

An evocative symbol

Schoolchildren from local primary schools usually enjoy coming into the church to have a thoroughly good look around and find out more about Christian worship. They are intrigued by the ancient nooks and crannies and enthralled by the story of Jesus' passion, which I recount with bread and wine as we are all gathered around the holy table. Some of the children are so small that they can barely lift their chins over the table-top!

At the font, which is full of shimmering water, everybody's imagination runs riot. 'What does water mean to you?', I ask –

and have often needed to stop the flow of ideas before they have come to an end, so great is the number of thoughts aroused in their minds. Water is so very fundamental to our lives that it is no wonder that it also has the capacity to evoke powerful associations.

How much water?

'My God is so big!' sings the all-age congregation at a morning service, everyone throwing their arms widely apart to demonstrate. God *is* big, and his faithfulness is so secure, his generosity so prodigal and his loving mercy so overflowing that we find it hard to imagine the scale of it all, let alone attempt to express it.

One way of helping us to do this, however, is to use our symbols in a generous and abundant manner. Using a mean amount of water from a little dish sitting at the bottom of a great big font says nothing about the magnitude of God's love for us, nor does it give the impression that baptism is terribly significant.

Baptism is an event of life-changing significance. It is a momentous rite of passage, something that is intended to leave its mark for the rest of one's life. Let's make a splash, quite literally, and use copious amounts of water if we can. We need not be afraid to make a lasting impression on either the candidate or the polished floor. Isn't this one of the Church's primary activities – making disciples and baptizing them?

The notes to *Common Worship*: Holy Baptism give us the following instruction:

> The use of a substantial amount of water is desirable; water must at least flow on the skin of the candidate.
>
> *Note 12, Holy Baptism*

Baptism, of course, is valid however little water we have; we will invariably come across situations where little water is available or using gallons of it is impractical. But this need not be the norm.

Fonts, baptisteries and salad bowls

It is easier for some churches than for others to use plenty of water. I have seen some fantastically innovative fonts. A church which I remember from my childhood had a font from which the water overflowed into a pool and then into a channelled stream which ran through the length of the church and outside into the world beyond. Nowadays we seem to be moving in two directions simultaneously. Recognizing an increasing occurrence of adult baptisms, in some places large fonts and baptisteries are being installed where the buildings can accommodate them. At the same time, there is increasing use of relatively small stainless steel bowls and similar vessels. The rationale for using these is that they are portable and can be moved with a minimum of disruption and fuss into a position of best visibility for the congregation.

A few weeks ago I visited a church in a local Urban Priority Area. We joyfully celebrated the baptism of a lively little three-year-old, using water from a bowl on a table at the front. The whole thing nearly went flying on a couple of occasions, because the lad first tugged at the table-cloth under the bowl and then grabbed hold of the bowl in an attempt to have a good look inside. Afterwards the family posed for photographs around the font – yes, the great old stone font which had been totally ignored throughout the service!

Some of our churches have fonts which are inaccessible or in cramped conditions and alternative solutions have been found, such as using a portable font. But there is much to commend the use of old stone fonts where these exist, not least because they can hold a lot of water (but we do need to fill it to the top) and are also constantly there to remind the Christian community from week to week of their own baptism and its implications. A portable bowl is swiftly moved out of the way and will appear again only when it is time for another baptism. It cannot induce memory from a cupboard. So let's take the lid off the font, wipe out the dust, replace the perished plug and give it a go!

Swimming pools?

What can we do if we definitely want to use the water symbolism to its full effect, we have adult candidates but we are hampered by insufficient facilities in our building? Here are a few ideas:

- hire the local swimming pool for a couple of hours;

- borrow a portable immersion font;

- borrow a neighbouring church which does have a baptistery and take the whole congregation with you;

- hire a 'birthing pool' – like a paddling pool, only much sturdier;

- build your own! This is not as impossible as it sounds. Others have worked temporary wonders with a few bricks, pond liner and a water heater.

Each of these ideas has its pros and cons, but in the end it may benefit our churches and the local community to try out some new ways of seeing and doing baptism.

Administration of the water

If we are convinced of the benefit of using plenty of water then we will probably want to make the most of it. Once we know how much water we are using, we then have to decide how we are going to administer it.

Once or thrice?

A threefold administration is the preferred option – dipping the candidate into the water or pouring water over the candidate three times. This is an ancient practice and emphasizes the threefold nature of the Trinity in whose name the candidates are baptized. A single dip or pouring is also permitted, however.

Dipping or pouring?

We can 'dip' or 'pour', but whichever we choose, we should not be sparing with the water. Baptism by immersion is still very much a novelty to many of us and, when we do come across it, it is mainly of adults and older children. It may come as a surprise, or even a shock, to learn that it is not unheard of to baptize babies and infants by immersion, too (although some parents might be hesitant to volunteer their precious offspring for this). And when we start to delve into church history, we might discover why our ancient fonts really are big enough for a baby to fit inside . . .

> Then the priest shall take the child into his hands . . . and he shall dip it in the water.

> But if . . . the child is weak, it shall suffice to pour water upon it.
>
> *Publick Baptism of Infants*
> The Book of Common Prayer 1662

The cross

When Cranmer simplified the symbolism in his baptism service, he maintained the Signing with the Cross, to the disapproval of other reformers of his day who thought that nothing should be allowed to detract from the symbol of the sacrament, the water. In the ASB the signing was given two optional positions: one at the Decision, where it has been traditionally associated with exorcism and protection from the powers of evil; and the other after the baptism, following Cranmer.

Common Worship follows *The Alternative Service Book 1980* and the options we are given are slightly different. Thus we may position the Signing with the Cross:

either

- at the Decision

or

- after the Baptism.

We must make the sign of the cross at least once in the service, and the recommended position is at the Decision. But take care: the accompanying words are not the same at both points. Signing before the baptism has a different association, traditionally, from the signing after the baptism. What we say with the signing of the cross at each point reflects this.

45

Signing with the Cross at the Decision

The signing at the Decision, as already indicated, is in the context of turning away from the devil and turning towards Christ. Its origins lie in a pre-baptismal practice in the Early Church. Catechumens (people preparing for baptism) were marked as Christ's own, no longer belonging to the powers of evil, after they had decided to turn to Christ. Later, St Augustine taught that the sign of the cross 'had the same protective value as the blood of the passover lamb on the doorposts of the children of Israel' (quoted in E. C. Whitaker, *The Baptismal Liturgy*[2]).

We can see traces of these roots in the words we use at this point:

Do not be ashamed to confess the faith of Christ crucified.

All **Fight valiantly as a disciple of Christ
against sin, the world and the devil,
and remain faithful to Christ to the end of your life.**

May almighty God deliver you from the powers of darkness,
restore in you the image of his glory,
and lead you in the light and obedience of Christ.

All **Amen.**

Signing with the Cross

A new option for parents, godparents and sponsors

After the candidates have been signed with the cross by the minister, parents, godparents and sponsors can also be invited to make the sign of the cross on the candidates. This can be a very moving action, expressing their involvement and identification with the step being taken. It makes no difference whether the candidate is a child or an adult.

Signing with the Cross after Baptism

Although signing with the cross may be appropriate after the baptism, the words which belong to a pre-baptismal rite are not. Instead, we make the sign of the cross with the words of the post-baptismal prayer of anointing:

> May God, who has received you by baptism into his Church,
> pour upon you the riches of his grace,
> that within the company of Christ's pilgrim people
> you may daily be renewed by his anointing Spirit,
> and come to the inheritance of the saints in glory.
> All **Amen.**
>
> *Prayer after Baptism*

Misleading actions

There is a popular or 'folk' misconception that the signing of the cross after baptism is actually the baptism itself – something along the lines that the cross of Christ = the christening. This is a belief that is only confirmed by ministers who dip their finger or thumb into the font before making the sign. The notes in *Common Worship* make it very clear that we should take care to make a signing after the baptism a quite separate action from the baptism itself.

Oil

Anointing with oil is a practice that goes back well into the Old Testament and, in common with other symbols, it has a multitude of associations and uses. Oil is gaining in popularity across the traditions in the Church and is used in a variety of circumstances, from deliverance and healing ministry to prayer with anointing for the gifts of the Spirit.

In *Common Worship* oil may be used with the sign of the cross in either (or both) of the 'signing' positions – see above. Since the anointing and signing have different significance depending on their context in the service, we are encouraged to use two different oils:

- oil of baptism (sometimes known as oil of exorcism)
- oil of chrism.

Oil of baptism

Oil of baptism is used at the Decision and this is usually a simple olive oil.

Commentators on baptism in the Early Church saw an anointing at this part of the service in terms of protection from the devil and preparation for the contest between Christian disciples and the spiritual powers, so graphically described by St Paul in his letter to the Ephesians:

> Our struggle is not against enemies of blood and flesh, but against the rulers, against the authorities, against the cosmic powers of this present darkness, against the spiritual forces of evil in the heavenly places.
>
> *Ephesians 6.12*

They also used the image of a contemporary athlete, who would have anointed his body with oil before a contest:

> From that day [of baptism] onwards, you will confront [the devil] in battle and this is why the bishop anoints you as athletes of Christ before leading you into the spiritual arena.
>
> *John Chrysostom (354–407), Baptismal Homilies 2.24*[3]

This sort of symbolism does not always work in our culture, although reaction to it is very variable. Most people, however, have a very deep-seated desire for God's protection from evil, both for themselves and for their children. Anointing with the sign of the cross at this point reinforces for the candidate and reminds us all of the protection that we are given by virtue of Jesus' death and victory on the cross. The priest then prays for deliverance, protection and direction:

> May almighty God deliver you from the powers of darkness,
> restore in you the image of his glory,
> and lead you in the light and obedience of Christ.
>
> *Signing with the Cross*

Oil of chrism

Oil of chrism is often fragrant, because it has perfume or spices mixed into it. It is used if we anoint after a baptism.

Put simply, this action is an anointing into the royal priesthood of all God's people, reminiscent of the anointing of kings, priests and prophets in the Old Testament, and a symbol of the empowerment of the Holy Spirit, equipping us for the ministry which lies ahead.

> You are a chosen race, a royal priesthood, a holy nation, God's own people, in order that you may proclaim the mighty acts of him who called you out of darkness into his marvellous light.
>
> *1 Peter 2.9*

How do we anoint?

There is no hard and fast way to do this. Some people use a special oil dispenser, rather like a sophisticated version of the sponge they use in Post Offices to moisten stamps. Other people keep the oil in a small bottle and simply tip it up on to their finger or thumb.

Then make a + sign firmly and deliberately on the forehead of the candidate.

If you are anointing with oil after the baptism, and have already made the + sign on the candidate at the Decision, a different sort of cross sign can be used at the anointing – the chi-rho. A chi-rho is a chi (X), a diagonal cross, superimposed with a rho (P). These are the first two Greek letters for the word *Christos*, meaning 'the Anointed One'. Make the sign of the chi first, then make the rho on top in one sweep, starting at the bottom of the stalk, going upwards and over the top in a loop. In actual fact, however, it is not essential to make any cross sign at all. It is the oil that is the symbol at this point and not the shape of it.

 Practical tip for ministers: anointing with oil leaves greasy fingers, so remember to have something at hand on which to wipe them afterwards. A helpful server or member of the congregation could pass both the vessel of oil and a purificator at the appropriate moments.

How much oil?

In the section on water we considered how using generous amounts of it can help the symbol to recall the abundance of God's goodness. The practice of a church in America, recorded on video as an educational aid (*This is the Night*, LTP, 1992, distributed in the UK by McCrimmon), has invariably raised comment in this country and it is worth recounting what they do at their anointing after baptism.

Instead of using a little dab of fragrant oil, they pour a warmed jug of it over the candidate's head! The oil runs down their face and neck and is rubbed in a bit, too. When the candidates on the video were interviewed afterwards, they said that the aromatic scent lingered for days and had contributed enormously to an experience which they would never forget.

> It is like the precious oil on the head, running down upon the beard, on the beard of Aaron, running down over the collar of his robes.
>
> *Psalm 133.2*

Where can we find this oil?

Most dioceses have a special service on or around Maundy Thursday each year at which the bishop blesses oils for liturgical use. They are then distributed and taken out into the parishes. If there isn't such a service in your diocese, then you can use your own oil, set apart for the purpose with a prayer of blessing.

Light

Darkness and light: one of the most evocative contrasts known to humankind. As surely as day follows night the symbol of light will retain its potency.

The ASB introduced the possibility of giving a lighted candle after baptism and the *Common Worship* services build on this. The most significant change, however, is that the recommended position for giving the candle is now at the end of the service, as explained in Chapter 1.

The new services also give a clear indication that 'a large candle' may be lit at the beginning of the Decision. If your church has a paschal candle then this is the obvious one to light. Many churches are not in the regular habit of using candles, but they might like to consider having a special candle for this occasion.

The smaller candles given to the newly baptized can then be lit from the flame of the larger one; the light of the risen Christ is passed on to his disciples as they are sent out in mission.

Where should we put the paschal candle?

If you do use a large, or paschal, candle then it is clearly an integral part of the baptism liturgy and needs to be where the rest of the action is. An obvious place is by the font. If the Decision takes place some distance from the font, however, then it would be more sensible to place the candle at the place of decision, which will probably also be a more sensible place from which to light the smaller candles at the end.

The candle could be carried in a procession to the font at the point of baptism and then returned to a more accessible position afterwards.

 Practical tip: don't forget to have matches (and taper) at the ready for lighting the candles.

Lay participation

The candles give an opportunity for some of the lay people in the congregation to play a part. Somebody needs to light the large candle at the Decision and give the lighted candle at the end. The ordained ministers do not have to be the ones doing this. It might be a job for the servers but it could equally be a task given to churchwardens, older children, or people who have been involved in the baptismal preparation.

Clothing

I wonder what St Paul thought about clothes and attire. He certainly paid enough attention to them to regard them as a good illustration; he mentions them in his letters to a number of churches; for example:

> Clothe yourselves with compassion, kindness, humility . . . clothe yourselves with love
>
> *(Colossians 3.12,14).*

> Put on the Lord Jesus
>
> *(Romans 13.14).*

> Put on the whole armour of God
>
> *(Ephesians 6.11).*

Putting on Christ, as though discipleship were something to be worn as a garment, is very much part of baptism. Using it as a symbolic action when a wet, newly baptized individual comes out of the water makes a lot of sense. This is a new feature in *Common Worship* and here is how it can be done:

- Place a garment (possibly a white robe, or perhaps a towelling gown) around the newly baptized person and use the accompanying words at this point.

- If they can remain warm and comfortable, they can stay like this until a later opportunity to get changed, possibly during a long hymn.

- Alternatively they could get changed immediately after the baptism, during a hymn. The words for the clothing can then be used once they have reappeared.

The accompanying words are very simple, using St Paul's words in his letter to the Galatians (3.27):

> You have been clothed with Christ.
> As many as are baptized into Christ have put on Christ.

The newly baptized individual does not need to be thoroughly wet in order to be clothed or changed, nor does he or she need to be an adult. I have heard a bishop suggest that a baby should be brought to baptism in its more ordinary clothes and changed into a glistening christening robe only after the baptism (which may, of course, be by immersion). The baby could be changed during a hymn and the words for the clothing could then follow after that. I'm not sure that most of the parents I come across would be ready to cope with this – but it gives us something to think about.

Needless to say, these new words after baptism make sense only when there is an actual 'clothing'. When there is no such symbolic action then the words should also be omitted.

All too much?

In the face of all these symbols, some of us will be throwing our hands up in horror, sensing a creeping intrusion of distracting ceremonies whose only effect will be to detract from the essence of the initiation service.

We are not obliged to take any of these new options on board, but we are invited to consider them seriously in the context of our renewed breadth of understanding about baptism. The only symbols that we have to use are those of *The Book of Common Prayer*: water and the sign of the cross.

If we are careful in choosing our options and the symbols that will enhance the worship of our local community, then we shall find that there is something there for everyone.

3 Enhancing the imagery

In this chapter... we shall explore some ways of communicating God's marvellous grace by non-verbal means and investigate ways of being more creative in presenting our baptism services.

The singing began in the large meeting room but, immediately, it began to move through the doors and out on to the path beyond. The musicians played their instruments as they were led through the grounds and across the little bridge that crossed the river. The music didn't stop until everyone had reached that spot, crowding the river banks and hanging over the side of the bridge to watch the young man and a couple of ministers in the water below.

After the baptism everyone returned to the meeting room, singing all the way; there they joyfully celebrated Holy Communion and went on their way into the rest of the day.

Occasions such as this are not easily forgotten. This is an account of baptism during a summer youth camp at which a young man from Liverpool committed his life to Jesus. The camp took place in a Quaker boarding school, which had no font in its meeting room. Using the river which flowed through the grounds seemed the most obvious thing to do.

We thought about water – how much to use, and so on – in the previous chapter. I'm not going to dwell on that, because it was not so much the river itself which stuck in my mind, as the mass exodus from the building and the march to reach the river. The movement and the sense of purpose and anticipation were absolutely electric!

Part of the reason for the vivid nature of the recollection is the way that the baptism was enhanced by an enactment of the imagery.

Imagery in *Common Worship*

The Introduction has already given us a very full account of the baptismal images included in the *Common Worship* services. The Bible contains a host of different ways of looking at baptism, so great was its significance to the New Testament Church.

In rediscovering some of the forgotten imagery, we deepen the quality of our worship. Good symbols operate on many levels, launching a multitude of connections and associations within a community. If we were to limit the perspectives on baptism to only a few images, we would be denying the multifaceted nature of the symbol. Instead, by using a number of biblical metaphors, we are saying that some people have seen it this way, while others have seen it like that . . . There are a myriad of valid perspectives and they all help to build up the picture of God's amazing work.

In addition, the metaphors and images we express in words can have a similar effect to that of symbols; breathed into by the Spirit, they draw us into deeper knowledge and experience of God.

Using imagination

It is not the intention of this chapter to dissect every available image in *Common Worship*. My main purpose is to encourage creativity in planning initiation services.

The God of imagination and inspiration has made us in the divine image; hence we have enormous resources at our disposal as we plan and prepare worship that will draw people into the very presence of God and will reflect something of the momentous character of baptism itself. We are, so often, reluctant to do anything out of the ordinary. As a result, we play down the dramatic nature of God's saving love, we understate the awesome wonder of standing in God's presence and we sell short the power and the glory of our creator. At baptism we are standing at the very brink of heaven; how could that ever be ordinary?

We have already found a few ways of enriching the imagery in the previous chapter: using plenty of water, for instance, or making something more of the 'clothing'. In the next few pages we shall explore a couple of images to build upon as we think through and prepare for our worship:

- Light

- Journey

Light in the darkness

Have you ever been up before the dawn and stepped out into the freshness of a new morning to watch the sunrise?

Think of the crowds wandering around our cities all through the night of 31 December 1999, waiting for the dawning – quite literally – of a new millennium.

On occasion, many of us will have stayed up through the night in a vigil of prayer, or waiting by a bedside, watching over someone who is terminally ill.

At times like these, the light in the East, first pale, next rich and colourful, then full and bright, stirs deep emotions within. We know that the rising sun is a powerful symbol in itself, and we can take advantage of this by incorporating it into our worship. There is more to light in a church than candles, and we shall consider the way that we can use natural light to its best advantage in baptism.

Those who watch for the morning

One of the traditional times for baptism in the Church's year is at Easter, most specifically on Easter Sunday. In the service described below, baptism takes place in the context of the Easter Vigil and Service of Light.

The service begins in the dark. The members of the congregation have either been there all night or have got out of bed in the small hours of the morning in order to attend. The building is barely lit at all; there is just enough light to prevent people from tripping up over the flagstones and furniture and to read a Bible; the atmosphere in the semi-darkness is one of quiet prayer and reflection. Sitting in the shadows, the congregation has recounted from Scripture the story of God's salvation history, from the creation of the earth in the book of Genesis and through the Old Testament. The readers stop short before the Easter passages because they will come later. Between the readings there is plenty of space, for no-one is in a hurry, everyone is waiting patiently, waiting for the risen Christ.

If the timing is right, then it is still mainly dark, with just a faint glow in the sky, as everyone moves through the church and out of the door into the chilly air beyond. As the dawn begins to break, a fire is lit and, from that, a large paschal candle. Everyone has been holding an unlit candle and now the light is passed on from the paschal flame, one to another.

By now the natural light is growing stronger, the congregation all have their own lights, and everyone returns to the inside of the building to hear the Easter readings from the New Testament and to rejoice in the resurrection of Jesus Christ, the bright Morning Star.

This is a wonderful setting for initiation! The paschal imagery is brought to life, of course, but so is everything about darkness and light. As the sun rises in the sky, so we celebrate the rising of the Sun of Righteousness. We baptize disciples into his risen life and they, too, are called out of darkness into God's marvellous light.

God has delivered us from the dominion of darkness
and has given us a place with the saints in light.

Giving of a Lighted Candle

If your church hasn't ever been up all night or before sunrise waiting for Easter to dawn, then all this might sound a bit far-fetched. But we think nothing of having a midnight communion service at Christmas and usually find that the building is packed out, even at such a seemingly unsociable hour. It is certainly worth a try. There is an order for an Easter Vigil in *Lent, Holy Week, Easter* and there will probably be one in the *Common Worship* Times and Seasons material when it is published. The baptisms, confirmations (if any) and congregational renewal of baptismal vows are followed by Holy Communion and all are dismissed joyfully. This could be an excellent opportunity for a parish breakfast, too, when the congregation can spend further time celebrating with the newly baptized.

Churches which do have a regular Easter Vigil might invite other parishes to join in and make something more of the occasion. Also, if there is to be a confirmation in the service, it will probably be easier to invite the bishop to a deanery or cluster initiation than to make a case for him to visit a single parish.

The humble electric light

We won't all be up at the crack of dawn on Easter Day and, even if we are, it's unlikely that we would be baptizing on that day to the exclusion of all other Sundays. There is still plenty of scope for enhancing the darkness/light imagery in the service, particularly when we have baptisms in the evening or our church buildings are naturally rather gloomy in the daytime when the electric lights are not on.

There is no fixed blueprint; we need to investigate our lighting systems and discover what we can use. Very few churches have only one light switch controlling all the lights. Usually different parts of the building can be lit separately. We may also discover a range of different lighting: some shining downwards, some into the roof, some strong, some soft, some providing a spot or pool of light on an area of particular significance, some on dimmer switches, and so on. There is plenty of versatility – we just need to mull over the possibilities and dare to try them out.

This use of special lighting aims to improve our worship and not to produce a crude, gimmicky effect. Therefore we need to bear the following in mind:

- thorough preparation is essential;

- whatever is done must make sense of the liturgy and not be intrusive or distracting;

- everyone involved in the operation of the lighting needs to be well briefed and rehearsed.

People on the move

The image of a journey is excellent as a metaphor of our Christian discipleship. It speaks not only of the way that we are but also of our roots in Judaeo-Christian tradition. It reflects the nature of our constant voyage of discovery as we travel through life, learning together about God. It also reminds us that from the time of Abraham, when God entered into a covenant and instructed Abraham and his household to pack up and go, God's followers have been a people on the move. We can trace the movements of God's people through much of the Old Testament, in the life of Jesus, in the spread of the New Testament Church, and in the struggles of the Early Church.

The complacency which enveloped the Church in this country when we settled physically into sturdy buildings during times of ecclesiastical prosperity and security has sometimes disguised the itinerant nature of our discipleship. We have been given an imperative to 'go', by a God who calls us to follow the Way and sends us out in mission.

The Church is still on the move, and we see this most dramatically in congregations which plant churches in school halls and new buildings. However, we can all do more in our worship to remind us of our nomadic status, wherever we meet; this is particularly true of baptism.

Processions

As a fairly young member of a church choir, my experience of the major feast days was of singing interminable hymns while we swayed our way around the aisles of our little Norman building in ingenious patterns and figures of eight. The congregation stood stock-still in the middle of it all, attempting to sing along but never quite sure whether to join in with the organ or with the men at the back of the procession, who always sang at full blast and never managed to keep in time with everyone else.

We had something of the right idea. We were expressing movement in our worship – but we were not actually going anywhere, and we were not doing it terribly well. Movement and procession do not have to be like that; there are ways of processing as a church which are meaningful and enjoyable for the whole congregation.

> Movement is the hallmark of a community which knows it has not arrived, but is in transit, discovering God not at the end of the journey but in the journeying. We move because we must.
>
> Richard Giles, Re-pitching the Tent [1]

Many churches with a number of robed personnel, such as servers, choirs, clergy and readers, have regular processions at the beginning and end of the service. This, too, makes reference to a journey. But what about the congregation? Where are we going? And how does all this apply to baptism?

Going somewhere?

Using the *Common Worship* Initiation Services and rethinking our theology of initiation gives us the opportunity to reassess the way we use our buildings for baptism. How much freedom we have may well depend on the amount of space we have in comparison to the amount of furniture and the number of people in the congregation. Let us consider a number of situations.

Lots of space for movement and a flexible building

It is a tremendous asset to have a building large enough to create distinct spaces with different focal points. If we are able to have space in special areas for

- gathering before and at the beginning of the service,

- the Liturgy of the Word,

- the Baptism,

- communion

and each area is big enough to accommodate everybody present, then the whole congregation is able to move from point to point along the journey with the candidates.

The service could begin in an entrance hall or a narthex for the Presentation of the candidates. The congregation could then all move to the place of baptism. The whole assembly progresses *en masse* through the building, sometimes standing in a gathered crowd (around the font or the altar, for example), sometimes pausing for a while on some chairs (sitting for the Liturgy of the Word, for example).

This sort of procession can have dignity and purpose without having to be highly choreographed or show the precision of a practised choir. We need not be so hung up on 'order' that we lose the spirit of the occasion. With clear instructions and firm leadership, people will soon grow used to doing something different, and if there are servers and a choir, then they could lead the way. Strategically placed sidespeople can give further encouragement to those who lack the confidence to move.

Lots of space but not many distinct areas

Recently I was invited to preside at a baptism in a neighbouring church whose vicar was ill. I visited the church in advance of the service to see the building and talk through the service with the Reader and a churchwarden. The building was massive; the chairs for the congregation filled less than half the nave at the front and the great font stood proud yet redundant in its own space right at the back, near the entrance door.

In this particular setting it would probably not have been terribly practical for the congregation to gather anywhere at the beginning of the service other than their usual places in the nave. There wasn't an obvious gathering place. It would have been ideal, however, if the congregation had moved *en masse* to the font at the baptism. There was plenty of room around the font where people could stand; the font was raised up, so visibility would be good; and there was quite a distance to walk from the chairs in the nave to the font at the back, so everyone would appreciate the sense of going somewhere. Adults and children alike could enter into the excitement of setting out on an expedition!

In fact it wasn't the right time for the church to change its practice of using a tiny little portable font by the chancel step. I was only a visitor, and the permanent font had been used as a stand for flower arrangements for so long that it would have taken more than a few days to smarten it up for use again. But it stands as an example of the potential that lies before many of us;

we merely need to step back and look at the building with a fresh perspective.

Not much spare space, but different focal points

The situation here is the church which is so full of people that there simply isn't room for everyone to move around. Or else a building that is so full of fixed pews that they have the same effect. Even the very largest churches can have this problem when they are full of people.

The best thing to do here is to preserve or create plenty of space within the significant areas of the building, so that ministers, candidates and sponsors can move from one point to another even if the rest of the congregation have to watch all the movement. The most the congregation can do is swivel on the spot and face wherever the action is taking place, but the effect of the movement will still be important.

No room to move

Some churches are absolutely packed to capacity for baptisms and there is not a spare centimetre of space in the building. There is no question of the whole body of people making their way over to the stone font in the corner by the door. There is barely room for a candidate and supporters to squeeze into the area!

On top of that, visibility is at a premium. The font is strategically positioned right behind an enormous pillar. This is where the temptation is greatest to have a portable font handy so that it can be placed at the front of the congregation – somewhere in the middle where more people can see it.

There is no simple solution to this. If you are still interested in incorporating some movement into the service, then I suggest that you select a group of people and take them into the empty building to dream some dreams about reshaping the interior. Then you set out on the path to re-ordering!

Worshipping in a hall, and other spaces

Worship in a hall, whether it belongs to a school or a parish, can be hard work. For a start, you have to begin afresh each week to recreate the required atmosphere and environment. You need to unload your equipment and set out the furniture from scratch. You have to work hard to disguise the PE equipment and, from week to week, you never know whether the artwork on the walls is going to be for us or against you. Praise God for the term when the school's project on Ancient Egypt coincides with your series on Moses!

Although this environment provides plenty of scope for versatility, elaborate layouts take a great deal of energy. By the very nature of the arrangement with the other users of the building, everything has to be temporary. A large permanent font is out of the question. Here are a few suggestions:

- Using the font that you have, create a regular place for it.

- Set up an area for baptism apart from the space where the congregation usually sits, so that there can still be an element of movement to the font.

- Construct a distinctive space around the font. It could have the same 'backdrop' all the time: a large dividing screen, for example; a set of specially designed banners; or perhaps an extensive drape of fabric carefully pinned to the boards on the wall. It needs to be something simple enough to put up and take down without much effort.

- Use the font in this position whenever there are baptisms and introduce an element of mass movement into the service.

In this way you can create more of a culture of baptism. The font becomes a more familiar feature and its presence whenever the church meets speaks of the importance and centrality of baptism.

In general . . .

 Practical tips for a 'moving' congregation:

- Rehearse all the ministers, servers and choir. A conspicuous body of robed people leading by example needs to be confident in its role.

- Brief the churchwardens and sidespeople. They will need to know what is expected of the congregation and be strategically placed for prompting people into motion at the right time.

- Rehearse the candidates and supporters as well. It's not fair to expect people to stand up in front of a congregation if they haven't had the opportunity to have a walk-through.

- Think carefully about where people are going to sit. In particular, keep candidates, sponsors, parents and godparents together. Reserve their chairs or pews with stickers or notices, if necessary. One parish church presents candidates with their lighted candle during a hymn, after which the appropriate words are used for the action. A congregation has never laughed so much during the final hymn as the day when the churchwarden couldn't find one of the candidates! The families involved in the baptism were scattered all over the crowded building and the poor woman spent several verses pacing aisle after aisle with increasing anxiety.

- Give the congregation very clear instructions. Explicit rubrics in a printed order of service are ideal. Otherwise, make verbal directions unambiguous and try to prevent them from being intrusive.

- Make sure that children are able to see and are not hemmed in between taller adults who totally obscure their view. They can be invited to the front of the crowd, if they are willing to leave their parents.

- Provide some chairs for elderly or infirm people in areas where you are expecting most of the congregation to stand, and make sure that people with impaired mobility are not excluded.

In conclusion . . .

The circumstances surrounding the baptism that I described at a summer camp at the beginning of this chapter were exceptional. Regular parish worship will not be exactly the same, but this need not dissuade us from being more adventurous as we find innovative non-verbal ways of communicating God's story in baptism.

4 Seasons and alternatives

In this chapter... we shall investigate the material specially provided for Epiphany/Baptism of Christ/Trinity, Easter/Pentecost and All Saints. We are given some other options, too, and shall discover why and when we might choose to use them: responsive versions of some of the prayers and a shorter Profession of Faith, for example.

The liturgical revision that preceded the ASB introduced a novel concept in Church of England liturgy: authorized choices and options (albeit at a limited number of points).

Since then, *Patterns for Worship, Lent, Holy Week, Easter, The Promise of His Glory* and other (unofficial) publications have provided us with even greater choice of alternative texts, some of which have particular seasonal and thematic emphases.

The Appendices

The *Common Worship* Initiation Services build on this practice. We are first provided with a complete order of service and the normal texts to use, and are then given a variety of extra material from which to choose if we wish. This extra material is found in the Appendices and falls broadly into four categories:

- Seasonal alternative material

- Other alternative material

- Lectionary

- Additional material

Seasonal material

The seasonal provision in the Appendices to the *Common Worship* Initiation Services consists of:

- Introduction

- Collect

- Prayer over the Water

- Peace

- Prayers of Intercession

- Prayer after Communion

- Blessing

for each of the following:

- Epiphany/Baptism of Christ/Trinity

- Easter/Pentecost

- All Saints

In different parts of the world and at different times in church history, baptism has been associated with particular festivals. We have largely lost sight of this because neither the BCP nor the ASB gave any seasonal preference for baptism, and we baptize all year round, without variation.

Easter/Pentecost

By the fourth century, Easter was considered to be *the* occasion for baptism. Pentecost and other festivals were sometimes alternatives but most baptisms took place at the Church's great primary festival. At Easter the candidates gained the full impact of sharing in Christ's death and resurrection, the image of baptism in Romans 6.

> We have been buried with Jesus by baptism into death, so that, just as Christ was raised from the dead by the glory of the Father, so we too might walk in newness of life.
> *Romans 6.4*

The Easter Liturgy in *Lent, Holy Week, Easter* reflects the practice of the Early Church by suggesting a Vigil of Prayer and Scripture – possibly through the night, followed by a Liturgy of Light, possibly at dawn, the Liturgy of Baptism and the Liturgy of the Eucharist. The full extent of the Easter Liturgy is not found in the *Common Worship* Initiation Services, but the seasonal alternatives for Easter and Pentecost bring out the paschal element of baptism as a particular feature and are entirely suitable to be used in that context.

The Easter/Pentecost alternatives are appropriately used at any time throughout the Easter season (Pentecost being the conclusion of the season in the *Common Worship* Calendar).

Epiphany/Baptism of Christ/Trinity

The feast of Epiphany originated in the Eastern Church as a celebration of the manifestation of God in Jesus Christ. It became associated with three themes: the Nativity (including the visit of the Magi), the Baptism of Jesus and the Wedding at Cana. The Baptism of Christ lent itself naturally to being linked with Christian initiation, and by the fourth century Epiphany had become a normal day for baptism.

In the *Common Worship* Calendar, Epiphany is both a feast day (6 January) and a season – beginning on the feast day itself and ending on 2 February with the Presentation of Christ in the Temple. The Baptism of Christ, a festival, is normally located on the First Sunday of Epiphany, unless Epiphany itself falls on a Sunday. Either way, both of these occasions are appropriate for baptism.

The proximity of Epiphany to Christmas and our celebration of the nativity will, of its own accord, give us a perspective on birth and new birth that is different from that of Easter. In *Common Worship* the emphasis of the seasonal alternatives for Epiphany is to recall Jesus' own baptism and underline the work of the Holy Spirit. And, since the baptism of Christ is essentially trinitarian – the synoptic accounts of the baptism being some of those rare biblical occasions where all three persons of the Godhead feature at the same time – this set of alternatives for Epiphany is particularly suitable for Trinity as well.

> Jesus . . . was baptized by John in the Jordan. And just as he
> was coming up out of the water, he saw the heavens torn
> apart and the Spirit descending like a dove on him. And a
> voice came from heaven, 'You are my Son, the beloved; with
> you I am well pleased.'
>
> *Mark 1.9-11*

The Promise of His Glory provided us with an extravagant
celebration for the Baptism of our Lord, drawing on all the
Epiphany themes and combining within them the possibility of
baptism. Many parish churches will consider a celebration of
Epiphany on such a grand scale to be beyond their capabilities or
preference. Others will be able to do them well, especially
cathedrals, which have plenty of space for movement around the
building and for gathering around focal points, and which are
well practised in large and special events. They could issue an
open invitation to other churches in the area to join with them.

It is likely that this kind of imaginative material will be included
in the *Common Worship* times and seasons volume which will be
published in due course.

All Saints

The special material for baptism at All Saints reflects the
eschatological nature of the feast day and the hope into which we
are all baptized. There is much to remind us of 'so great a crowd
of witnesses' which surrounds us, as described by the writer to
the Hebrews. Reflection on the road trodden by so many who
have gone before us in the way of faith will encourage us.

Fill these waters, we pray, with the power of [the Holy] Spirit,
that all who enter them may be reborn
and rise from the grave
to new life in Christ . . .

As the apostles and prophets, the confessors and martyrs,
faithfully served you in their generation,
may we be built into an eternal dwelling for you . . .

from the All Saints Prayer over the Water

Although the seasonal material has been provided for special use at appropriate seasonal times of the year, any of these options can be used at any time. So if the All Saints choices are particularly suitable for a Sunday in the middle of August, for example, then we are at liberty to use them.

Other alternative material

- Responsive forms of the Prayer over the Water

- Prayers of Intercession

- Profession of Faith

- Questions at the Decision

Responsive forms of the Prayer over the Water

A substantial amount of our baptismal theology is located within the Prayers over the Water. It is no surprise, therefore, that these prayers have to be fairly lengthy, even when the full breadth of the imagery we want to use is distributed between four different versions – the prayer for general use and the three seasonal ones. The responsive forms in the Appendices offer us an approach which is more engaging for members of the congregation and should help them to stay more involved and connected with the prayer than they might be if they tend to drift off during priestly monologues!

There is a responsive form available for each of the four Prayers over the Water. The main text of each prayer remains the same and the congregation comes in at a number of points, usually at the prompting of a recognizable phrase spoken by a minister or sung by a cantor or choir (see overleaf).

Using a responsive form does, of course, mean that members of the congregation need more words in front of them, particularly with the Epiphany/Baptism of Christ/Trinity version in which the congregational response has no trigger. The whole prayer would have to be printed out in a service booklet or on a notice sheet.

General
Lord of life,
All **renew your creation.**

Epiphany/Baptism of Christ/Trinity
(between phrases of the prayer, without a cue line)
... we give you thanks and praise.
... Lord, receive our prayer.
... Alleluia. Amen.

Easter/Pentecost
Saving God,
All **give us life.**

All Saints
Hope of the saints,
All **make known your glory.**

Prayers of Intercession

All together there are five different forms for the Prayers of
Intercession. One is in the main text of the service, three are
seasonal variants and the fifth is in an appendix. They all draw
on different images and biblical phrases, and we simply need to
find the one most fitting for each particular occasion.

Most members of our congregations will probably not have
access to the omnibus version of the Initiation Services. On the
whole, the only people who need the total provision will be
ministers and Readers who are preparing and leading services.
We will consider the options for congregational orders of service
in Chapter 5. It is worth commenting at this point, however, that
those of us who have the books and the full range of material
must take care not to withhold these five alternatives from our
intercession leaders inadvertently. We need to equip them for the
task they have been given; it might help to produce a little
booklet for intercession leaders containing the different versions
from the master volume.

Intercession leaders need not use any of these set forms at all, of
course. They can create their own prayers, pray extemporarily, or
even lead a period of open prayer. The beauty of the set forms,

apart from the fact that they have been carefully written to reflect the themes and images already present in the service, is that they provide a ready-made framework for busy people when time and creative inspiration may be at a premium.

Profession of Faith

The normal Profession of Faith used in the *Common Worship* Initiation Services is the Apostles' Creed. This is an ancient baptismal tradition of the Church and its regular use will remind us of one of our most fundamental Christian texts. Fewer and fewer younger people ever go to a service in which the Apostles' Creed is recited, and using it at baptism is a good way of getting the text well and truly into our memories. Many people, however, valued the shorter profession of faith in the ASB, finding it more easily accessible to the families bringing infants and children for baptism.

The alternative Profession of Faith now in the Appendices to the *Common Worship* baptism service has been written along the same lines as the ASB version. It has a little more substance yet retains its short, pithy questions in a trinitarian form. This alternative is permitted 'where there are strong pastoral reasons'; exactly what those strong pastoral reasons might be has been left to our own discretion.

Questions at the Decision

'Strong pastoral reasons' might also indicate that the ASB questions at the Decision are more suitable than those in the main text of the *Common Worship* services. When the *Common Worship* services were originally authorized, this alternative text was not available; it was provided subsequently as an option, following calls from various quarters.

Lectionary

The lectionary for Holy Baptism contains biblical references in the following categories:

• Readings generally appropriate for baptism

- Suggested readings for baptism 'seasons'

- Readings for a vigil or post-baptismal liturgy

- Canticles in Procession to the Font

Help! Which lectionary should we use?

We have already been given a new and complete lectionary in *Common Worship: Calendar, Lectionary and Collects,* and now we are being given another one for baptisms. Which lectionary has priority over the other?

Before we can answer that question, we have to ask ourselves two preliminary questions relating to the specific baptism service we are planning.

- When in the Church's year will this baptism take place?

- Is the baptism part of a regular Sunday service or does it hold a special significance as the major 'theme' of the whole service?

Answers:

- If baptism is to be part of the regular Sunday pattern, and it is seasonal time, i.e. from the First Sunday of Advent through to the Presentation of Christ, or from the First Sunday of Lent to Pentecost, or a principal feast, e.g. Trinity Sunday or All Saints, then we would usually use:

  > the appointed Collect of the day;

  > the normal Sunday readings.

- If the baptism is part of the regular Sunday pattern but in Ordinary Time then:

  > we could use a baptism collect instead of the collect of the day;

  > we would still use the normal Sunday readings.

  In this way we need not disrupt the flow of semi-continuous Bible reading as provided by the *Common Worship* lectionary, or our own scheme of Bible readings (now permitted at specific times of the year). This is particularly pertinent to parishes which hold baptisms in their main Sunday services every few weeks.

- If the Sunday baptism is a 'stand alone', special event, and if the theme of the whole service focuses on baptism, then it would make sense to use the baptism collects from *Common Worship* and choose from the readings and collects in the Appendices.

- The same answer applies if the congregation is coming together for baptism on an ordinary weekday; a baptism collect and readings from the Appendix would be very suitable.

NB These guidelines apply to the lectionary choices only. The other seasonal alternatives (for example, the Introduction and the Prayer over the Water) can be used at any time of the year, regardless of the readings or the context of the baptism.

Vestments and colour

The guidelines relating to choices from the lectionary will also apply to liturgical colours.

Basically, if the baptism is set within an otherwise normal Sunday service, we continue to wear whatever colour is normally appropriate for the day.

If baptism is the principle feature of the service, however, it would be appropriate to wear a baptismal colour. White is popular, although some people prefer red with its connotations of the Holy Spirit. At Epiphany, Baptism of Christ, Easter, Pentecost, Trinity and All Saints we are likely to be wearing these colours in any case.

Readings for a vigil or post-baptismal liturgy

Although we are given some readings, we have neither a vigil nor a post-baptismal liturgy in which to use them! We may well have to wait for the publication of further material, provisionally called *Rites on the Way*, which will contain services and prayers surrounding baptism.

Canticles in Procession to the Font

Naturally these are likely to be most useful to churches with a strong choral tradition and those whose normal custom is to have processions from one part of the building to another. Churches with bands and music groups, which never sing the psalms or which struggle with small congregations who can barely keep a tune going, might be tempted to dismiss these psalms and canticles entirely.

> With joy you will draw water from the well of salvation. And you will say on that day: Give thanks to the Lord, call on his name; make known his deed among nations; proclaim that his name is exalted.
>
> *Isaiah 12.3,4*

Don't disregard them immediately, however, if your church is of a very different ethos. In actual fact, the biblical canticles are worth looking at because they form the basis of a number of hymns and modern worship songs with which you might be familiar. Even cathedrals have been known to sing one or two of these!

And if the words of the psalms are unfamiliar, have a look at the back of some hymnbooks and songbooks. Many of them have appendices connecting hymns with Scripture passages; these could give you some new ideas.

Conversely, if your church does have a strong choir which is accustomed to doing all the psalm-singing, then hymns and songs derived from these canticles could give your whole congregation the opportunity to raise their voices as everybody makes their way joyfully to the font.

Additional material

- Thanksgiving Prayer for a Child

- A Litany of Resurrection

Thanksgiving Prayer for a Child

The 'Thanksgiving *Prayer* for a Child', located in the Appendices to Holy Baptism is not to be confused with the *Service* of 'Thanksgiving for the Gift of a Child', which is completely different and will be discussed in Chapter 7 of this book.

The Thanksgiving Prayer is exactly what it says it is: a short and simple expression of thanks and wonder for a new child, intended to be used in the context of a baptism service. It should be inserted right at the beginning of the service between the Greeting and the Introduction. If the baptism is the first occasion on which the family has been able to share publicly their little bundle of joy (and heartache!) with the church community, then it is highly appropriate for the congregation to share in a prayer offering thanks to God and asking for his support in the years to come.

This prayer is an optional provision; it will not always be necessary or desirable to use it. The family may have already participated in a service of Thanksgiving for the Gift of a Child, for instance. Time constraints might also indicate that it is best excluded.

A Litany of Resurrection

This litany is one of the suggested canticles which can be used in procession to the font. It is printed out in full because, unlike the other canticles, it is not straight from a biblical text but is rather a combination of biblical and credal phrases.

Take time to discover what's here

All in all, there is an absolute wealth of material to be found in the Appendices, and they are well worth looking through for ideas that will suit your church.

5 Which service do we use?

In this chapter... we shall have a look at the structure of the services and consider the questions we need to ask before we can decide which initiation service to use in our situation. We shall also consider some of the order of service options available to congregations and address the question of 'wordiness'.

Let us imagine four very different initiation services.

Deanery confirmation at All Saints, a large suburban church

The deanery confirmation service is held twice a year, rotating through the churches in the deanery. It is a very special event and the host church has been preparing for weeks. Imagine the excitement and expectation: a packed building, dozens of candidates and their supporters, a well-rehearsed ceremony, choir or music group and ministers galore. The setting is spectacular, the music lively and the bishop is presiding. There is a buzz about the place and a strong sense of 'something happening'.

The candidates have come from all over the deanery. The young people have been prepared in a 'deanery group' whilst the adults have been prepared by their own parish churches. A number of the candidates have not yet been baptized, so there will be baptisms in the service too. The theme of initiation will be woven throughout the service, from beginning to end.

10.00 a.m. at St Edmund's, in a rural village

The baby boy brought for baptism this Sunday morning comes from a local farming family whose land stretches from the village right out to meet the main road at the top of the ridge. The baptism will be incorporated into the regular Parish Communion service. The family and friends of the little boy are given a warm welcome and invited to squeeze into the pews nearest to the font. There isn't a lot of space to spare in this tiny ancient building.

They don't usually have many children in the congregation – the primary school and uniformed organizations are invited along every now and again for special services like Harvest Festival and Mothering Sunday. Today, however, several children have come with the family for the baptism.

6.30 p.m. at St Anne's, a city-centre charismatic church

There is a large student contingent in the regular evening congregation of this church, and two of the candidates in this Sunday evening service are students reaffirming their baptismal faith, originally declared on their behalf at their baptisms almost twenty years ago. They were confirmed at around the age of twelve and now feel the need to express something further. There are also a couple of candidates for baptism: adults who have come through the weekly *Alpha* course. This celebration is in the style of their regular 'Evening Worship', a Service of the Word.

All the words for the service, the songs and the congregational texts, are displayed on a couple of OHP screens; there's a lot of singing at the beginning, with joyful swaying and clapping. Before the baptisms, which take place in a massive immersion font, the candidates recount their stories to the congregation and afterwards there is a lot more singing while candidates and minister change out of their dripping clothes.

3.00 p.m. at St Peter's, a parish church in a town centre

The priest at St Peter's is absolutely swamped by requests for infant baptism; even if he tried to hold them all during the main Sunday service, he would have to baptize every week in order to fit the regular congregation plus the visitors into the church building. He felt strongly that he did not want to go down the road of 'private baptisms', although he realized that he was going to have to hold some services on Sunday afternoons in order to deal with the sheer numbers. Armed with conviction, he enlisted the assistance of the Mothers' Union and the organist.

The women in the Mothers' Union were delighted to be involved in the process of baptism because they saw it as a practical outworking of their *raison d'être*. Many of them have now become involved as members of the baptism preparation team. They turn up for the baptisms with other members of the church and provide refreshments in the church lounge after the services. During the service there is organ music, well-known hymns and a great deal of life.

The shape of the services

It will be clear from these sketches that it is not necessary to use exactly the same service for each occasion; sometimes baptism will be in a Communion service, sometimes it will be in a Service of the Word, sometimes it will stand on its own. Sometimes a confirmation service will contain only confirmation, sometimes the service will also contain a baptism or a 'Reception into the Communion of the Church of England', and so on.

Whilst the context of initiation can vary from occasion to occasion, the underlying structure remains the same. The Introduction to the *Common Worship* Initiation Services explains the 'dramatic flow' of an initiation service, drawing us into the transforming presence of the living God. It provides the rationale for the structure of the *Common Worship* Baptism and Confirmation.

Within the dramatic flow of the service,

> the Church proclaims what God has done for his people in
> Christ and offers us a way of entering that movement from
> darkness to light, from death to life, from being self-centred
> to being God-centred.
>
> *Introduction to* Common Worship *Initiation Services*

The underlying structure of the service reflects this dramatic flow.
After the Greeting there is an opportunity for thanksgiving. The
Liturgy of the Word, which includes the sermon, proclaims God's
story and interprets the meaning of our own stories alongside it.
In response to the gospel, the candidates are presented for
baptism, they declare their renunciation of Satan and their
turning to Christ, and they are marked with the badge of the
Christian, the sign of the cross. At the font the minister prays
over the water and the whole Christian community professes its
faith together by saying the Creed. The candidates pass through
the waters of baptism and may be clothed and anointed. The
newly baptized are commissioned for their discipleship and join
the rest of the congregation for the Prayers of Intercession and
the action of the Eucharist. After the blessing, but before they
leave, the newly baptized are given a lighted candle with the
charge to 'Shine as a light in the world to the glory of God the
Father', and they are dismissed with the rest of the believing
community to do just that.

The structure is important, but it is only part of the picture. It is
designed to work alongside the texts themselves, the symbols,
imagery, music, silence, movement and action, to enable people
to experience for themselves the transforming nature of baptism
and the love of God who embraces them.

Two groups

In the *Common Worship* Initiation Services we find two groups
of services, each containing the basic structure described above.
There are also several derivative services which have been worked
out from them. The two basic services are:

- Holy Baptism (at the Eucharist): a single rite for children and
  adults.

- Baptism, Confirmation, Affirmation of Baptismal Faith and Reception into the Communion of the Church of England (at the Eucharist): a range of services recognizing that a person's spiritual journey does not always fall into one pattern.

A number of different services derived from these basic models may well suit our needs and save us from having to start from scratch when we are putting a service together. These are the services that have been worked out for us:

- Baptism outside the Eucharist

- Baptism of Children at the Eucharist

- Baptism of Children at a Service of the Word

- Emergency Baptism

- Baptism and Confirmation at the Eucharist

- Confirmation at the Eucharist

- Baptism and Confirmation outside the Eucharist

- Confirmation outside the Eucharist

- Affirmation of Baptismal Faith at the Eucharist

- Reception into the Communion of the Church of England at the Eucharist

There are also a few outlines provided for further possible situations, which are not written out in full; Baptism of Children at Morning or Evening Prayer, for example.

Despite the number of worked-out versions, they are not exhaustive, and we might well discover other possibilities more suitable for our own situation. What has been provided, however, will cover the most commonly used patterns and save us all a great deal of work!

Appropriate choice

What are the factors which determine our choices when we are faced with the provision in the *Common Worship* Initiation

Services? Before starting to plan a service we have to ask ourselves a few questions:

- *Is this a 'stand alone' initiation service or part of a regular pattern of Sunday worship?*

  The answer to this question might depend on whether the service is for baptism or confirmation. Confirmations are more likely to have initiation as the dominant element.

  It might also depend on how often we have baptism services. It is not helpful to allow the theme of baptism to distort the important rhythms of the Church calendar if there are baptisms every few weeks. If we do have a lot of baptisms in our main acts of worship, then it is usually best to incorporate them as a part within a greater whole, rather than sweep all else aside to concentrate on only initiation in the service.

  If we feel that we have no choice but to hold baptisms outside the main Sunday services, then these would clearly have baptism as the dominant feature.

- *If this is part of our regular pattern of Sunday worship, into which service is it to be integrated?*

  All the initiation services in *Common Worship* can be used with any usual Sunday service, whether it be a Eucharist, Morning or Evening Prayer, or a Service of the Word.

  The Prayers of Penitence are omitted and the normal Creed is replaced by the interrogative form of the Apostles' Creed, used immediately before baptism or confirmation. The Prayers of Intercession may also be omitted.

- *Which components will be incorporated?*

  We need to establish which of the following will be included: Baptism, Confirmation, Affirmation of Baptismal Faith, Reception into the Communion of the Church of England.

As we continue to plan the detail of the service we will need to ask:

- *Are the candidates adults, children or both? If children, are they old enough to answer for themselves?*

The baptism service is essentially the same whether the candidates are infants or adults. This is important, because it emphasizes that baptism has a single status, regardless of the age of the candidate. A six-week-old baby is just as fully initiated into the Church at baptism as a sixty-year-old grandmother. However, for obvious practical reasons, there are a few points in the service when things might be done a little differently:

➤ At the beginning of the service an optional prayer of thanksgiving for the child may be used, which can be found in the Appendices.

➤ At the Presentation, candidates who are old enough to answer for themselves (whether child or adult) may be asked if they wish to be baptized, and they make their reply. They might also give a testimony.

➤ The questions at the Decision are addressed to infant candidates 'through' their parents, godparents and sponsors.

➤ Immediately after the Profession of Faith, if the candidates are able to answer for themselves, the minister may ask them directly, 'Is this your faith?' and they reply, 'This is my faith'.

➤ The Commission for those who are able to answer for themselves is different from the Commission for those who are not.

• *Are we in a festal season?*

• *At what time of day will the service be?*

• *Who will be in the congregation?*

For example, will there be a lot of visiting children, or a large proportion of people who are not used to going to church and will not know our more recent hymns and songs?

• *How can we use the building, music, lighting, movement and so on?*

• *Who will be taking part in the service?*

Whilst not specifically pertinent to the planning of our service, we may wish to consider these further questions, as well:

- *If we have adult candidates for baptism and confirmation, and the confirmation is not in our parish church, where should the baptism take place?*

  Some congregations like to have their own candidates baptized in the parish church so that they can be initiated among those with whom they feel they belong. Often it is not possible to take many of the congregation to a deanery or diocesan confirmation, either through sheer restrictions of space or because of the distance.

  It makes much more sense, though, to have the baptism and confirmation in the same service if possible. As the Introduction to this book explains, initiation is complete in baptism and is the major rite of passage into the Church; it makes little sense to 'manufacture' a second climax to initiation a week or a month later, when the newly baptized adult will have to answer exactly the same life-changing questions all over again.

  In addition to this, the bishop is the principal minister of baptism in the Church. It is important that he is seen to fulfil this role by presiding over baptism and even to baptize whenever this is feasible.

- *Are our children regularly missing from baptism?*

  Unless we ensure that some baptisms take place in all-age services, or the children are kept with the rest of the congregation until after the baptism, or brought back just in time, then our children might always be in their groups while baptisms are taking place. If that is the case, they will be deprived of the opportunity to learn about the importance of their own baptism and even the realization that baptism is a feature of church life at all!

  It may be that we will need to reassess our patterns and practice – perhaps by ensuring that the children are brought in for baptism, or by changing the type of service altogether, for their sake.

Will the congregation have a book?

This is a question that has been vexing parishes for quite some time, and the answer is that it depends on your local church. Here are some pointers to the answer; this list is only a starter and other publications are bound to spring up from all over the place in the early years of *Common Worship*:

- *Common Worship: Initiation Services* is the 'omnibus' volume for worship leaders. It is not intended to be bought for every member of the congregation.

- The 'Sunday' book, *Common Worship: Services and Prayers for the Church of England,* contains the full version of Holy Baptism and extracts from the Appendices. The congregation has all the necessary words for baptism, but they may need to skip over some of the optional bits that you do not wish to use, and they may need to turn to the Appendices for some of the alternative choices. (There is no confirmation service since the book is intended for normal Sunday use.)

  Not every church will have copies of *Common Worship: Services and Prayers for the Church of England,* anyway, given the alternative possibilities.

- There is a Holy Baptism 'card' with appropriate congregational texts on it.

- There is a Holy Baptism booklet, containing the minister's words as well as those for the congregation. Some, but not all, of the Appendices are included.

- An increasing number of churches are producing their own order of service booklets or service cards. They can then devise their own style and have exactly what they need. *Visual Liturgy, Common Worship* text disks and access to the Internet have made this approach so much simpler for churches which have a computer and a photocopier. Booklets can be made as disposable or as long-lasting as required, depending on the quality of the paper, the cover and the binding. Once you have the equipment, production is relatively economical. It has to be said, though, that costs can mount up and local production is not always cheaper than using officially published materials.

Mark Earey has written a helpful book for churches wishing to go down this path, entitled *Producing Your Own Orders of Service*.[1]

Not all churches have the necessary technology for this. If this is your predicament it would be worth having a word with your Diocesan Liturgical Committee to ask whether they, or another liturgically-minded computer buff, would be prepared to provide a range of templates for parishes to buy into, or even to operate a service whereby they prepare orders of service for individual parishes.

- Those churches which use overhead projectors nearly all the time will find that it is possible to use the same computer technology to produce high-quality acetates. Ensure that a couple of other potential weaknesses do not let you down, however: the positioning of the screen, and untrained people controlling the projector and acetates. If you are to avoid detracting from the worship then these issues need to be approached with careful thought and preparation.

One particular point needs to be looked at when using a screen for a baptism service: what happens if we have our backs to it when we are facing the font, or if we are singing whilst moving around the building?

- When it comes to confirmation, you are likely to have to produce a local edition. This is not usually the sole responsibility of the local church, however. The bishop and his liturgical advisers will have to decide how to proceed.

They may decide to have a single diocesan version, set up to cover all eventualities and wheeled out for every confirmation service. The difficulty with this approach, of course, is that it would be hard to incorporate the seasonal variety and reflect the flexibility within the *Common Worship* services. You would either end up with a 'fixed' version that never used alternative options, or you would have to include the options in the booklet, either within the service or in some appendices, and be in danger of losing the flow.

It may be preferable for someone in the diocese to make a number of templates available. There could be several different diocesan sets made up, depending on the components and season. Another way of approaching the question is to appoint a diocesan adviser with responsibility for printing orders of service for each distinct event. The advantage of this arrangement is that everything specific to the service can be put into one booklet, including the hymns and songs and the names and parishes of the candidates.

Worried about wordiness?

When the *Common Worship* Initiation Services were first authorized there were complaints from many quarters about 'wordiness'.

Over the past twenty years there has been much complaint regarding the (allegedly) flat, inexpressive language in the ASB, and attempts had been made to address this by enriching the language in all the new services. The richer imagery in the new baptism might be more pictorial and incorporate more biblical ideas, but it is also more complex and conceptually challenging. Ministers who felt that the supposedly 'banal' language in the ASB was, in actual fact, more accessible to their congregations felt let down by the new baptism service. In this regard, it would seem that the Liturgical Commission just cannot win.

At the same time there was concern surrounding the length of the texts in the *Common Worship* baptism service. The number of questions at the Decision had been doubled, for instance, and the short Affirmation of Faith had turned into the full-length Apostles' Creed. There were also some extra bits, such as the prescribed number of readings and the Commission.

It is not all compulsory

The Liturgical Commission and the General Synod have taken all this on board and have addressed the problem since the first publication of the Initiation Services. Some parts of the service, once mandatory, are now optional and we can decide for ourselves which of them we should or should not include. There was already quite a lot of optional material in the service; we need to look carefully at the notes and rubrics for guidance. Then we can include only the sections which are mandatory and those which will suit the occasion.

Mandatory and optional sections

Which parts of a service are required to be used will depend on the type of service in which a baptism is set. In a main Sunday service, Baptism at Holy Communion will, not surprisingly, have more compulsory content than Baptism at a Service of the Word. A 'stand alone' baptism, in which the baptism is the sole theme and focus, will have yet different constraints.

Whatever the context of the baptism, however, the following sections of the service are optional:

- Prayer of Thanksgiving

- Introduction

- Some of the readings preceding the Gospel

- Hymns, songs, psalms and canticles

- Presentation of the Candidates (i.e. as covered by the opening rubric in this section; the questions in this section still remain)

- Lighting a large candle

- Additional Signing with the Cross by parents, godparents and sponsors

- Clothing

- Anointing with oil

- Commission (although it needs to be paraphrased at some point, if the candidate is an infant)

- Prayer(s) at the Commission

- Prayers of Intercession

- Greeting the newly baptized/exchanging the Peace (the corresponding action is optional, but not the words)

- Blessing

- Giving of a Lighted Candle

It is most unlikely that many of us would wish to exclude all of these optional features from the same service. Some of them we would never want to omit; other parts we might leave out only for pressing reasons, on rare occasions. But at least, given these choices, we have the scope to put together a service which best meets the needs of our candidates and congregation.

Shorter forms

In addition, where there are 'strong pastoral reasons', the shorter forms of the following may be used:

- Questions at the Decision

- Profession of Faith

The alternative questions at the Decision are as in *The Alternative Service Book 1980,* and are not printed in the 1998 edition of Initiation Services (they were authorized by General Synod for inclusion at a later date). The shorter Profession of Faith is in Appendix 7 of Initiation Services.

Recently, I went to a baptism in a cathedral. They did the whole baptism service, including a mass movement of 300 people to the font and back. It was also a service of Holy Communion, so we had all the typical choral inserts and a substantial adult sermon; the 300 people moved, again, to the altar and back, and it was still over in an hour and fifteen minutes. It need not take nearly as long in a parish church, if we do not want it to.

Other ideas

The curious thing is that the actual words of a baptism service do not take very long to read through out loud. Wordiness is often a matter of perceived length rather than actual length; the music and silence, the ebb and flow of the action, things that we look at and smell and feel – they all affect our perception of the passing of time in worship. So here are a few other things we could try in order to make the words more interesting.

- How about speaking over well-chosen music, to create a different effect? As a background to the Prayer over the Water, for example.

- Integrate the sort of ideas about light found in Chapter 3 with the spoken word.

- Use the responsive forms of the Prayer over the Water.

- Use different voices to share out the words – for the Prayers of Intercession or the Commission, for example.

- Use *The Dramatised Bible* for the readings.[2]

- Sing a hymn or song while people are moving around the building; waiting can feel rather dull otherwise. Or break up a hymn by verses; sing some on the way to the font and the rest on the way back.

- Try using visual images at some points, with a slide projector or overhead projector acetates.

The way a particular service will turn out is very much up to us to decide. God will fill our earthen vessels with his Spirit (we hope) and the worship will come to life. But it is up to those who plan and prepare the services to give some form to those vessels by crafting the tone and feel. There is much flexibility in the *Common Worship* Initiation Services and there should be no reason why we cannot find exactly the right options for our own situations, different as they all will be.

6 Confirmation, Affirmation and Reception

In this chapter... we shall take a brief look at three pastoral rites closely related to baptism.

Much that has been written about baptism in the earlier chapters of this book will also apply to Confirmation, Affirmation of Baptismal Faith and Reception into the Communion of the Church of England, for the meaning of these services is derived from baptism and they remind us of our baptismal status and journey.

These services are the most 'official' amongst the range of possible services for use with people at different stages of their pilgrimage. Confirmation requires the presence of a bishop, and it will often be appropriate for the other two services to be integrated with confirmation while the bishop is in the area. These *Common Worship* services reflect their baptismal roots clearly in their structure, their use of baptismal texts and the way they encourage us to be at the font for the Profession of Baptismal Faith, whether or not there are to be baptisms in the service.

Confirmation

As the Introduction to this book makes clear, the position of the Church of England on the role and purpose of confirmation is still under debate. *On the Way* is a significant General Synod report from 1995 which researched and formulated approaches to Christian initiation and looked at ways of integrating patterns of evangelism and nurture with the liturgy of initiation. The report identified three distinct patterns of Christian initiation running concurrently in the Church of England today.

- In one pattern, people are baptized as babies and are confirmed as older children or teenagers, confirmation being the gateway to Holy Communion.

- In the second pattern, people who come to faith as adults and have not been previously baptized are baptized and, subsequently, confirmed. (Confirmation may be later in the same service, or on another occasion.)

- In the third pattern, babies and children who are baptized are admitted to Holy Communion on the basis that their baptism is complete sacramental initiation (although they usually have to wait until they reach a certain age). Confirmation comes much later, when the individual is ready to make an adult declaration of his or her faith.

(The House of Bishops' guidelines of March 1997 anticipate that children should be around the age of seven or have a certain appreciation of the eucharist before they are admitted to communion. If, however, the 'gateway' to communion is baptism, then the imposition of further conditions are considered by many to be unnecessary. Other denominations, most notably the Eastern Orthodox Churches, admit the baptized to communion from infancy, placing a tiny crumb of bread on the baby's tongue and a drop of wine poured from a spoon.)

Each pattern raises questions about the services we currently use.

The first demands that confirmation precedes Holy Communion, and this is in accord with the traditional Anglican two-stage view of initiation. This view was supported in the late nineteenth and early twentieth centuries by the argument that there was an original, integrated initiation service, of which baptism and confirmation were the two parts, and which has since become disintegrated. In this view, initiation was incomplete without confirmation – hence the two stages. Since communion was to be partaken of only by full members of the Church, communion was to be withheld until after confirmation. More recently, however, scholarly and ecumenical consensus considers that this is not the case, and that initiation is complete in baptism.

The second pattern demands that adults baptized in advance of a confirmation service have to make a repeat performance of their declarations and profession of faith, devaluing the unique nature of the first.

The third pattern has yet to be worked out in the light of experience, but the fear is that people will think that confirmation is generally unnecessary and, as a result, bishops might end up with a declining role and decreasing opportunities to meet their flock. The role of confirmation continues to be under scrutiny and the *Common Worship* services do not attempt to pre-empt any particular conclusion:

> The confirmation services . . . follow carefully traditional
> Anglican practice and make no attempt to resolve these
> difficult questions.
>
> *Commentary*
> Common Worship *Initiation Services*

It continues to be the discipline of the Church of England that individuals baptized in adulthood should be presented for confirmation before they can be full communicant members.

> There shall be admitted to Holy Communion:
>
> members of the Church of England who have been
> confirmed in accordance with the rites of that Church or
> are ready and desirous to be so confirmed . . .
>
> *from Canon B 15A*

It is not within the scope of this book to make a thorough critique of the current situation nor to review confirmation as a practice. Whichever pattern of initiation the local church is following, however, *Common Worship* contains material that is fitting and relevant.

Affirmation of Baptismal Faith

St Anne's, the city-centre church described towards the beginning of Chapter 5, has two particularly striking characteristics.

The first is that a large number of students attend the evening services. The Christian students return to their universities and colleges to interact with other students, many of whom are at a point in their lives when they are exploring the meaning of life. It is not surprising that some of these young adults, hearing the gospel afresh or for the first time, are intrigued, come along to discover some more about Jesus and, in time, commit their lives to following him.

The second characteristic of this church is that baptism is very dramatic. Before they had an immersion font, they would hire part of the local leisure centre on a Sunday afternoon and a large proportion of the congregation would go along for the baptisms. Now they have the font, filled chest-high with water, a prominent focal point to the service. Baptism is undoubtedly a major event and visitors to the service cannot fail to be challenged to a greater or lesser extent by the drama which they witness.

The combination of these two characteristics brings about a common question from a particular group of young adults. They are people who were baptized as infants and confirmed as adolescents and who, subsequently, became disenchanted with the Church and left. On rediscovering their faith in a new context, they have a desire to make a public act of commitment which equals the significance of those baptisms. 'Please can I be baptized again?', they ask. The inevitable answer, of course, is that both baptism and confirmation are unrepeatable.

Until now parish clergy have had to answer this question with a negative, having no substantial positive alternative to offer. The Affirmation of Baptismal Faith recognizes the need for services which mark a variety of stages along the journey of faith and for a service which provides an opportunity for significant public affirmation of faith beyond confirmation.

This is an extremely useful pastoral service. It can be used in the context of baptism or confirmation, though this is not absolutely necessary, because it can also stand on its own within any regular church service or as a special event. There is no absolute need for a bishop to be present and the service can be presided over by a priest.

Affirmation of Baptismal Faith, a significant public opportunity for individuals desiring to mark a major staging post in their journeys of faith, is a service to be used sparingly. It is not to be confused with a more frequent Renewal of Baptismal Vows, such as that used by whole congregations all over the country, often on Easter Sunday.

Corporate Renewal of Baptismal Vows

Both the main *Common Worship* book and the President's edition contain a form of congregational Renewal of Baptismal Vows. Essentially this is for occasional use – no more than once or twice a year – within a service other than a baptism or confirmation. Drawing on texts from the Initiation Services, members of the congregation answer the questions at the Decision and profess their faith in the words of the Apostles' Creed. The Affirmation of Commitment (from the adult Commission) may also be used.

If the congregational Renewal of Baptismal Vows does take place within a baptism or confirmation, notes to the service suggest that the responses of the people follow the responses of the candidates at the Decision:

President	Do you reject ...
Candidates	I reject ...
All	**I reject ...**

from Corporate Renewal of Baptismal Vows

Reception into the Communion of the Church of England

Since confirmation remains a requirement in the Church of England for people baptized as adults, any adult joining the Church of England from a non-episcopal church will still have to be confirmed. This includes Methodists, Baptists and members of the United Reformed Church. The Canon which was quoted earlier goes on to address people from other denominations who regularly come to the Church of England over a long period of time:

There shall be admitted to the Holy Communion: . . .

[persons who have been] otherwise episcopally
confirmed with unction or with the laying on of hands

from Canon B 15A

People who are considered to have been so confirmed need only
to be 'received' into the communion of the Church of England
should they desire to become members. This includes Roman
Catholics. However, the definition of episcopal confirmation is
more complicated these days, with an increased number of
confirmations by priests in the Roman Catholic Church and the
Nordic Churches of the Porvoo Agreement. There is also a
question about presbyteral chrismation in the Eastern Orthodox
Churches. Life is never simple! If in doubt, ask your bishop for
advice.

Gestures

There is a striking difference in gesture between this service and
confirmation and affirmation. In confirmation the bishop first
prays for the candidates with his hands outstretched towards
them. He addresses each person by name, saying:

> N, God has called you by name and made you his own.
>
> *from Confirmation*

He then lays his hand on the head of each candidate, saying:

> Confirm, O Lord, your servant with your Holy Spirit.
> **Amen.**
>
> *from Confirmation*

Similarly, in affirmation the bishop first prays for the candidates
with his hands outstretched towards them. He then lays his hand
on each person's head, saying:

> N, may God renew his life within you
> that you may confess his name this day and for ever.
> **Amen.**
>
> *from Affirmation of Baptismal Faith*

At reception, the bishop prays also for those wishing to be received with his arm outstretched towards them. After this, however, the bishop does not lay his hand on them but, instead, takes the hand of each person to be received, with the following words:

N, we recognize you as a member of the one, holy,
    catholic and apostolic Church;
and we receive you into the communion of the
    Church of England
in the name of the Father, and of the Son, and of
    the Holy Spirit. **Amen.**

from Reception into the Communion of the Church of England

Taking someone by the hand is an affirming gesture of welcome and partnership, more appropriate to this particular step in the journey of these particular people.

It is not absolutely necessary for the bishop to be present at Reception into the Communion of the Church of England (although it might be desirable), unless the individual being received is a priest. In this case the priest from another denomination does have to be received by the bishop. But in any event, whether the person being received is an ordained or lay person, and whether the bishop is to be present or a Church of England priest is sufficient, the reception may be more or less of a public event, depending on individual circumstances. There is no hard and fast rule.

These services – Confirmation, Affirmation of Baptismal Faith and Reception into the Communion of the Church of England, the last two of which are new – help us to make more sense of the reality we face. Coming to faith, growing in faith, returning to faith, changing church and other milestones along the way are all part of the journey we travel, but they should not all be marked in the same way. In these services we now find greater adaptability in celebrating the significant steps which people have taken. By having more choices available, we have more appropriate means of meeting the pastoral needs with which we are presented.

7 Thanksgiving for the Gift of a Child

In this chapter... we discover what this re-titled service is like and look at some examples of how it can be used.

It is not always easy to have children. I have had a relatively straightforward passage into motherhood; yet, even so, when my first child was born she was not the culmination of my first pregnancy. A few years later, and only minutes after my third baby had been delivered, he collapsed in my arms, flopping even more than a normal newly-born. He had stopped breathing. Emergency medical staff swarmed into the little room as if from nowhere and all I could do in my hopelessness and despair was to urge my bewildered husband to pray. With skill and equipment our son was revived; our relief was immense. Brought face to face with the fragility of life, we were reminded once again that a child is a precious gift from God, and we were profoundly thankful.

> Children are a gift from the Lord;
> they are a real blessing.
>
> *Psalm 127.3,*
> Good News Bible

For some, stepping into parenthood is as simple as slipping on a pair of moccasins. For others it comes only after years of waiting, sometimes accompanied by pain or sorrow. For some it will come through adoption. There will be parents who had given up hope of ever having a child, having explored every possible avenue without success; and there will also be those for whom parenthood comes as a surprise or a shock.

Whatever else it may be, for most people the arrival of a child is utterly life-changing. The soft, warm, vulnerable creature evokes within us an enormous sense of responsibility; it challenges our priorities, makes irresistible demands upon us and turns our lives around to the extent that we are never the same again!

The service of Thanksgiving for the Gift of a Child is for any parent or parents longing to express some of these feelings before God. It helps us to articulate our thanks and wonder at the miracle of birth. We ask for God's blessing on the child, for growth and strength in mind, body and spirit. We also pray for God's help in the responsibilities of parenting in the years ahead.

Whilst the thanksgiving service is not, strictly speaking, an initiation service and need not be used in conjunction with initiation services at all, it can come into the category of services surrounding baptism. It is most certainly a significant asset to the Church in terms of baptism policy and a few notes about it are included here for this reason.

Background

The ASB services Thanksgiving for the Birth of a Child and Thanksgiving after Adoption signalled a radical departure from the BCP's The Thanksgiving of Women after Childbirth (commonly called the Churching of Women). The ASB had a revised emphasis on thanksgiving for the child and turned away from the focus on the woman and the connotations of 'purification' after childbirth.

Both the ASB and *Common Worship* thanksgiving services are clearly distinct from baptism, and therein lies their value. How to distinguish between thanksgiving and baptism, and how they might be used in conjunction with each other, will be addressed later in the chapter.

Developments since the ASB

The *Common Worship* service builds on the ASB services, changing the title so that it encompasses both birth and adoption within the one service and can be more easily used with a child who is older. It retains its simplicity and structure, whilst having more substance with some additional elements. Experience of twenty years' use has resulted in some informed improvements, changes and additions. Here we shall summarize the differences between the *Common Worship* thanksgiving and the ASB provision:

- The *Common Worship* service covers both birth and adoption.

- The new service can be used more flexibly and has greater possibilities than before because its use is no longer restricted to a church building. The notes to the service explain that we can use the *Common Worship* service can be used for a number of different occasions:

  ➤ the private celebration of a birth or adoption, at home or in church with only family and close friends present;

  ➤ the public celebration of the birth or adoption of a number of children, perhaps in church on a Sunday afternoon;

  ➤ the public celebration of the birth or adoption of a number of children as part of a main Sunday act of worship.

  from Notes to Thanksgiving for the Gift of a Child

- There is a 'Pastoral Introduction', explaining the service. This can be printed at the front of the service booklet or card and the members of the congregation can read it through on their own before the service.

- In its minimal form the *Common Worship* service is short and simple. It can also be made more substantial by longer readings, more prayers and the addition of hymns and songs at suitable points.

- The Giving of a Gospel is now an intrinsic part of the service, and not just an option.

- A specific blessing of the child is now included.

- There is now a choice of readings, in addition to Mark 10.13-16. There is a list of possibilities in the appendix, but any suitable passage may be used.

- There are a number of optional features:

  ➤ Pronouncing the child's name.

  ➤ The presence of 'supporting friends and relatives' who may stand with the parents at the thanksgiving and present the child to the minister. They may give their pledge to do all they can to help and support the parents in bringing up the child.

The minister may address the supporting friends and say

Will you do all that you can to help and support N and N in the bringing up of N?
With the help of God, we will.

  ➤ The minister may also ask the wider friends and family to pledge their help and support to the child's family.

The minister may address the wider family and friends and say

Will you do all that you can to help and support
this family?
With the help of God, we will.

- The additional prayers which may be used in the service cover a wider range of possible circumstances than the ASB.

  For example, the *Common Worship* thanksgiving has optional prayers for the grandparents and other relatives, brothers and sisters, and the father. There are also new prayers which recognize that circumstances may not have been straightforward, such as the one which acknowledges a difficult birth. Another is a prayer for when the child has special needs. Prayers for health workers and the birth parents of an adopted child are also included.

- This *Common Worship* service is not designed to be used immediately before baptism, as the ASB service could be. The *Common Worship* baptism now contains an optional 'Thanksgiving Prayer for a Child' which is based on prayers from the Thanksgiving for the Gift of a Child; this can be used before the baptism.

- In order to emphasize the distinction between thanksgiving and baptism, and to save confusion and uncertainty in the future, the notes require a Register of Thanksgivings to be kept at church and a certificate to be given (see the section below on distinguishing between the two services).

Structure of the service

The structure of the Thanksgiving for the Gift of a Child is laid out below. The service has been put together in such a way as to be flexible enough to meet all possible situations. The starred items* may be used or omitted according to the circumstances and the minister's discretion.

INTRODUCTION

  Welcome and/or Greeting

  Praise*

  Collect

READING(S) AND SERMON

  Reading(s)

  Sermon*

THANKSGIVING AND BLESSING

  Presentation of the child*

  Prayer of thanksgiving

  The child's name is ascertained and pronounced*

Prayer of blessing (child)

Prayer that the child will come through faith and baptism to the fullness of God's grace

Prayer for the parents

GIVING OF THE GOSPEL

Presentation of a Gospel

Support to the family is pledged by . . .

supporting friends and family*

wider family and friends*

PRAYERS

For the tasks of caring and parenting

Additional prayers*

The Lord's Prayer*

ENDING

Blessing (whole congregation)

How much or how little goes into the service depends entirely on the context and the people involved. Obviously some prayers with the family in the front lounge at home will be more informal than during a communion service at church, however relaxed our worship!

Similarly, if the Thanksgiving does take place during a regular Sunday act of worship, then we must adapt the service according to the context. The prayer for God's blessing on us all is normally used as we 'round off' the service; it would not make much sense to have it twice in different places, for instance. Nor would we want to have the Lord's Prayer in the Thanksgiving section and again after the eucharistic prayer.

Distinguishing between Thanksgiving and Baptism

There will inevitably be people who confuse the two services of thanksgiving and baptism. Most are aware that baptism involves water, but the existence of other features in the thanksgiving which people associate with baptism can give the impression that this is actually happening, especially because a lot of people are, understandably, not familiar with the fine detail of the liturgy. Memories also fade over time and events merge in our minds. As a family recollects the big event, their baby's new outfit, all the relatives who were there, the vicar and so on, it is easy to be unsure of what the service was.

Be clear from the outset

The most helpful way to avoid confusion is to make people aware of the choices and distinction between thanksgiving and baptism from their very first enquiry, and make sure that what you say is backed up by any literature handed out, mentioning that there are two services and outlining the differences.

Naming

In folk tradition, the baptism is the occasion when a baby is given its name. This is not actually true. The child's name is given long before this, often on a little hospital tag around the baby's wrist. The name is subsequently registered officially. The rubrics of the BCP, in which the minister is instructed to say to the parents, 'Name this child', live on and, of course, we still use the name of a child as we baptize it, whichever form of service we choose.

It is important for some people that they have the chance to pronounce the child's name publicly, and this is provided for in the thanksgiving service. Given the link that this has with baptism, however, it will be important to make the distinction especially clear in the preparation.

Supporting friends and relatives

When a baptism is being planned, even before the service of thanksgiving takes place, the supporting friends and relatives may well be people who, in due course, will be godparents at the baptism of the child. Whether this is the case or not, it must be stressed that these supporters are definitely not godparents at this point, and will not be until the baptism itself.

Certificates and register

Once we have explained all the differences and made clear the distinctions, giving a certificate should put paid to any further misapprehensions regarding the type of service that has been attended by a family. The notes to the thanksgiving service instruct us to both give a certificate to the family and keep a register of thanksgivings in the church so that they can be kept for future reference in case any confusion should arise.

How can we use the service?

The notes to Thanksgiving for the Gift of a Child, quoted above, indicate a number of uses, each of which may vary dramatically from the others. Sometimes the service will be a private, quiet affair, maybe at the home of the family; at other times there might be several children brought to church by their parents after birth or adoption and the building will be packed with their friends and relatives. Here we expand upon some of the possibilities.

The thanksgiving service can be an integral part of a church's baptism policy, being offered as a preliminary and preparation for baptism. Some people will inevitably see this as a mere delaying tactic on the part of the Church, a hoop through which to jump before they can have what they really came for, the baptism of their child. But there will also be those who grow in the space and environment we create. There is a significant difference between the essence of the thanksgiving, which is a response to God's goodness in creation, and that of baptism, which is covenant and commitment. The one may lead to the other, but not usually immediately. The preparation will give time to reflect on the ultimate questions we confront at baptism and we may see parents making significant progress in their quest for meaning and God.

Alternatively, a church may plan to use the thanksgiving service, not regularly in this way, but only occasionally, when it is particularly apt. There may be parents who come asking for baptism yet recognize, after some investigation, that baptism really involves more Christian commitment than they can promise. They will be pleased to discover that there is another service that will exactly meet their needs. The thanksgiving service can then be arranged, either in a main service or in a more private context, at a time convenient for the family.

Another way that Thanksgiving for the Gift of a Child might be used occasionally is with committed members of the church who wish to give thanks for their new child at the earliest possible opportunity, before the whole congregation. The family may not wish to wait until the baptism before 'introducing' him or her to the church and saying special prayers. It need not be intrusive; in its most concise form, this will take up very little time within a Sunday service, yet it will be a moving moment for the fellowship, which may well have followed the development of the waiting, the hoping, the 'bump' or the adoption for quite some time.

Yet another purpose for the thanksgiving with committed Christians is to provide a Christian 'rite of passage' after birth or adoption for families who do not feel at all comfortable with infant baptism; they would prefer that their child should have the choice left open, to be able to make its own decision to follow Christ when it is older and to be baptized at that point. It is important for them to mark the birth with thanks and praise to the God who has given the gift, and they most certainly want to pray for God's blessing and guiding hand on the child's life. Again, the service can be in a main Sunday service, the family being surrounded by the church family and friends they know so well. In this situation we would probably include several of the optional features of Thanksgiving for the Gift of a Child, to make more of the occasion.

Three churches, and how they use the Thanksgiving for the Gift of a Child

Here are accounts of three churches, outlining their practice in the use of this service. They will not fit every church, but may provide inspiration.

The Living Waters Church Plant

The church, which meets in the local school, was created in order to reach the parts of the parish that the other churches didn't reach. The minister is well known in and around the school and he finds that he has several requests a year for baptism from families who normally have nothing to do with the Church.

During an initial visit, the minister discusses the differences between the thanksgiving service and baptism, and explains how one might suit the family's circumstances better than the other. If the family have never been to a service before, then he will always encourage them to come along to find out more. They are bound to know some members of the congregation, since several of them are also connected with the school, so this is a good start.

No interest in Church

If the family show absolutely no interest in venturing into the midst of the worshipping community, but are still very keen for their child to 'have a good start' by being blessed by a minister in the midst of a family gathering, then the minister will suggest a Sunday afternoon service, a Thanksgiving for the Gift of a Child.

The minister approaches the service with the same rationale with which he approaches the funerals and marriages of certain other people in the parish. These are people who have a deep-seated sense of wanting God to be involved in this important stage of their lives and know that this is most certainly what they must have, even though they are not ready for any level of commitment. If the minister can help people to meet God at times like this, then they might be willing to seek him further at another point. He knows that by setting up something on a Sunday afternoon he is separating these people from the majority of the worshipping community, but he also knows that people have been known to join the Church after attending a funeral or wedding that he has taken.

Congregational involvement

The church does not abandon the minister to these services. A number of the morning congregation turn up to welcome the visitors and settle them into the building. Some of them lay on tea and cakes at the back of the hall after the service, when they have a chance to have a chat. A brief encounter, maybe, but one to be followed up at the school gate in the weeks to come.

The Parish Church of the Holy and Undivided Trinity

Holy Trinity is a country church with a half-time priest-in-charge who lives in the village. The church has close links with the village school since the priest takes assemblies regularly and the schoolchildren visit the church for a special service with their parents once a term. There are also connections through the toddler service and frequent conversations on Main Street between the vicarage and the all-purpose Post Office. As a result of years of involvement, the priest and some members of the church have good relationships with the young families in the village.

As a result, many of the young families, whilst not all being regular church attenders, feel that they belong to the church and that it belongs to them. The priest takes the opportunity to build on this and, whenever she discovers that a new baby is expected, offers to visit and say a prayer with the family as the delivery draws near. She visits the newly-born infant at the earliest opportunity and asks the family if they would like to give thanks to God for their little bundle of joy. If they say 'yes', and at everybody's convenience, the priest returns for the little service. All gather in the living room – parents, baby, other children, sometimes with grandparents and close friends. The priest has printed out a short order of service so that everyone can see the words.

It is all over in just ten minutes but not forgotten by many. It is the sort of thing that people talk about for years to come.

St Hilda's Church

St Hilda's has a large congregation and a sizeable parish, and frequent requests for baptism are made at the 'Clergy Hour' in the Church Office by the parents of new babies. The church has a well-structured baptism policy and committed lay involvement in the preparation and follow-up of baptism families. As soon as a family asks for their child to be baptized, the clergy are able to make a welcoming and positive response. They take out their diaries and book a date for a Thanksgiving for the Gift of a Child, a service that is offered to everyone requesting baptism, whether or not they are regular members of the Church. The thanksgiving service will take place in the Sunday morning worship and the date planned is as soon as it is conveniently possible for all concerned.

Immediate response

The fact that the clergy are able to respond with a positive suggestion straight away means that the pressure is off them to explain all the 'ifs' and 'buts' of baptism before they have even had a chance to get to know the family. If the first thing a family hears – or thinks it hears – is that the church wasn't very keen to accept them and their baby, then there can be a great deal of hurt and misunderstanding. We all know from experience that people rarely forget these emotions, and angry tales of an unwelcoming church or vicar who 'wouldn't baptize my John' live on for a long time in a community.

The service of thanksgiving paves the way for a gradual introduction to the church. On the day, the congregation is welcoming towards the family and joins in wholeheartedly with the prayer after the minister has prayed for God's blessing on the child. After the service some of the regular members greet the family and make them feel at home.

As time goes by, the parents take part in the baptism preparation course. No dates for baptism are set initially, until the family are sure that baptism is for them. There is a weekly preparation course which runs concurrently with the Junior Church on a Sunday morning. The whole assembly starts together in the church building and, after ten minutes or so, the Junior Church and the baptism group move out of the church building and into the church rooms for their groups, all run by lay leaders. If the baptism families have other children then they are able to go along to the Junior Church too, or are taken to the crèche.

Not ready for baptism

Some people decide that they are not ready for the demands of baptism and are happy to settle for the thanksgiving service alone. Their needs have been met. Others will continue with the course. The final session is on the day preceding the baptism, when they meet in church with godparents and the minister who will baptize their child; they walk and talk through the service and ask any questions that are on their minds. By this time they will have laid the foundations for a number of relationships within the fellowship and the transition from the baptism group into the wider fellowship of the church will be one of progression and not a leap into the dark.

The thanksgiving service has played a major role in drawing people gently into the community of faith. It allows the Church to offer a service that will meet the initial needs of a family desiring to express their wonder and gratitude to God, to articulate their yearning for the very best for their child and to ask for help with their life ahead as parents. It can also help to prepare a more fertile ground in which the people of God can nurture the seeds of faith.

8 Ministers and ministries

In this chapter... we shall look more closely at the roles that ordained ministers have in initiation services.

All that we have seen of the *Common Worship* Initiation Services so far demonstrates the inclusive nature of initiation; it is an intrinsic part of the mission of the Church and, as such, the whole Church needs to be involved in the process in one way or another. We have also thought about some of the specific roles that church members might play in the preparation and nurture of candidates for baptism, some of which are brought out by words or actions in the services themselves. These might be godparents, sponsors and parents of infant candidates, for example.

Most churches have some regular lay leadership in main Sunday services. We have mentioned choirs, music groups and servers; lay people may also welcome worshippers on their arrival, read from the Bible, lead the assembly in intercessory prayer and give lighted candles to the candidates at baptism. We now turn to the role of ordained ministers.

A word about presidency

The terms 'president' and 'minister' crop up at different places all over the *Common Worship* Initiation Services. This is not an inconsistency; the distinction is deliberate.

Presidency at baptism is similar to presidency at the Eucharist and, indeed, if there is also to be a eucharist in the service then the president should preside over this as well. The task of the president is to hold the service together. The president gives the service a beginning and an ending and moves the service along, keeping it to shape by making a contribution here and there at significant points. Contributions to the service from other people are to be welcomed and often there will be many others involved in leading parts of the service. The president is not the president by virtue of the fact that he or she says the most; this may not be the case. What the president does, however, is give the service a sense of unity and continuity – rather as a 'continuity' presenter does in a news programme.

A congregation is greatly helped by having a sense of security created by the president, and leading worship does not have to be heavy-handed or excessively conspicuous to be firm. On the other hand, chaotic leadership, swapping from one person to another with no clear anchor point, can be quite distracting. I used to belong to a church at which the service leader would sometimes disappear for periods of time, leaving an empty space at the front. It felt very odd and it sometimes seemed as though we were in danger of losing the plot!

. . . and other ministers

It is clear in the Initiation Services that there is a place for other ordained ministers as leaders of worship. The president presides over the baptism, although others may baptize. This is achieved by the president saying the Prayer over the Water and leading the people in the Apostles' Creed, for instance, then another authorized minister of baptism may administer the baptism itself. The president would then continue by praying the prayer for the anointing of the Holy Spirit. Another example would be at the Decision: the president asks the questions, but another minister may make the sign of the cross on the forehead of each candidate.

Churches that are accustomed to distinguishing between the roles of president and deacon in Holy Communion will be familiar with this way of doing things and will slip into it easily. In parishes that are not used to this, it will take a little adjustment and some study of the rubrics to see how it can work. In any case, this new approach in *Common Worship* allows for a great deal more flexibility and freedom than the ASB, and removes the obligation for the presiding priest or bishop to do virtually everything.

Making the right signals

One of the questions we need to consider when there are a number of people up at the front is how to ensure that the president is perceived as such, even when she or he is passive. It is remarkable how something as simple as the positioning of the president's chair can make a difference to the message that is conveyed. We need to pay attention to detail. While it is extremely difficult for most clergy to find a Sunday when they can sit in the congregation, it does help to see things from a fresh perspective. We might never notice how ridiculous something looks from the pews, because we don't view the situation from that angle. It is also very useful to visit other churches and learn how they do baptisms. 'Dream on,' I hear some clergy cry, 'I have X number of churches and I'm the only ordained minister.' I wonder whether it would be possible for your deanery to redistribute its clergy and Readers temporarily from time to time in order to give each other this sort of opportunity.

If circumstances restrict you from doing either of these exercises, then you (and some others) could take time to sit in the church building and think through every aspect of the service, perhaps walking through some of it, imagining the impact of every movement and action and creating a vision of how it might be done even better.

The bishop

The bishop is the principal minister of baptism in the diocese. In effect he delegates baptism to his clergy because he just cannot be present at every baptism that takes place. Whenever the bishop is present at baptism, however, he should preside, whether the service is taking place in the cathedral or a parish church. By presiding over the sacrament whenever he can, he is able to demonstrate the reality of his role. Following the principles of presidency outlined above, if baptism is at Holy Communion then the bishop should preside over the whole service.

Parish clergy are still obliged to inform the bishop if they are intending to baptize an adult in their church:

Of the baptism of such as are of riper years

At least a week before any such baptism is to take place, the minister shall give notice thereof to the bishop of the diocese or whomsoever he shall appoint for the purpose.

from Canon B 24

Confirmation

The bishop also presides over confirmation; the *Common Worship* confirmation, just like the baptism, allows for ample delegation of various parts of the service, including the administration of the water at the baptism, if there is to be one in addition to confirmation. It is clear from the rubrics in the service which parts may be given to others.

Affirmation and Reception

Whilst the presence of a bishop is absolutely necessary for a confirmation, this is not the case for Affirmation of Baptismal Faith. Personal circumstances will probably indicate whether the Affirmation would be most appropriate in the presence of the bishop or not. Similarly, Reception into the Communion of the Church of England requires only a parish priest, unless the individual being received is an episcopally ordained priest from another denomination.

Priests and deacons

Priests and deacons are authorized ministers of baptism. When there are two or more ordained ministers in a service, they have an ideal opportunity to make a creative interpretation of the distinct roles of 'president' and 'minister'.

To summarize, there are distinctive roles to be played by ordained clergy and also possibilities for demonstrating a model of shared ministry between clergy themselves and between clergy and lay people.

In addition . . . lay ministers of baptism

In the case of an emergency 'life or death', situation, when no priest or deacon is available, any lay person may be the minister of baptism; there is a form for Emergency Baptism after the appendices in the *Common Worship* Initiation Services, if anyone can lay hands on a copy in such circumstances. In its most simple form, all that is necessary is that the minister pours water on the person being baptized, saying:

> I baptize you in the name of the Father, and of the Son, and of the Holy Spirit. **Amen.**

If circumstances permit, the minister may then say the Lord's Prayer and the Grace or a blessing. If time is not pressing quite so hard, a few verses from Scripture may be spoken before the baptism, the sign of the cross may be made and a few short prayers inserted. The baptism should be recorded.

Should the person so baptized survive the emergency, then they should subsequently be brought or come to church for a public service, similar to that of baptism, so that they can be received by the whole church. Instructions for such a service are also after the appendices in *Common Worship* Initiation Services.

Whilst there are some people in the Church who are campaigning for Readers to be able to baptize, lay people may still only baptize in cases of emergency.

9 Using the Initiation Services to prepare for baptism

> **In this chapter...** we select a few of the texts from the baptism service that particularly lend themselves to being used in baptism preparation. We consider how they might be used in the preparation of parents and godparents, older children and adults, and how the congregation can also prepare for the service.

A wander round any good Christian bookshop or resource centre reveals a whole range of baptism books and preparation courses for parents and godparents. There will also be enquirers' courses for adults and helpful evangelistic booklets explaining the basics of the Christian faith and answering some of those knotty questions. With the arrival of the *Common Worship* Initiation Services there are bound to be even more in the pipeline. It is not the intention in this section to offer an overview of available publications nor to weigh the relative merits of different approaches to Christian nurture. Here we shall merely identify some of the texts from the baptism service that may be useful.

Parents and godparents

When a congregation welcomes families for baptism month by month, only to discover later that many of them had little real intention of getting involved in the fellowship, it will be disappointed and frustrated. It will have to face the fact that the families have had totally different expectations and understandings of baptism from those of the regular members of the church. Sometimes the church has failed to communicate adequately and sometimes the families do not really want to know.

It takes time and patience for church members to build a trusting relationship with the family and explore with them their reasons for bringing their child to church. They may be several steps away from understanding their role and the nature of baptism, but when they do reach that point, looking at the questions at the Presentation may help.

First of all, we can assure the parents and godparents of the support they can expect from the Christian community, expressed in the question:

The president addresses the whole congregation

Faith is the gift of God to his people . . .
People of God, will you welcome *these children/candidates*
    and uphold *them* in *their* new life in Christ?
All **With the help of God, we will.**

from the Presentation

Then we can make clear the part they have to play:

Parents and godparents, the Church receives *these children*
    with joy.
Today we are trusting God for *their* growth in faith.
Will you pray for *them*,
draw *them* by your example into the community of faith
and walk with *them* in the way of Christ?

. . .

In baptism *these children* begin *their* journey of faith.
You speak for *them* today.
Will you care for *them*,
and help *them* to take *their* place
within the life and worship of Christ's Church?

from the Presentation

These questions make excellent discussion starters. They are packed full of pointers, and we can begin by eliciting a response on a very practical level:

- What sort of examples do we set our children?

- How can we help our children – or adult candidates, for that matter – to take their place within the life and worship of Christ's Church?

- How do we pray?

These questions could then lead on to some further discussion:

- What does it mean, to walk in the way of Christ? How do we walk in that way?

- How can we walk with our children in the way of Christ?

People who come to church regularly find it hard enough to articulate their faith. We are asking too much of families who are unfamiliar with the Church to give eloquent expression to their own experiences of God; we need to be gentle. These questions from the Presentation give us a helpful opening.

As the preparation progresses, it may be useful to concentrate on two or three images from the baptism service. We can unpack them together and investigate the sacrament from different angles. The Prayer over the Water is laden with baptismal images and holds our theology of baptism; this is a good place to look:

Over water the Holy Spirit moved in the beginning of
   creation.
Through water you led the children of Israel
from slavery in Egypt to freedom in the Promised Land.
In water your Son Jesus received the baptism of John
and was anointed by the Holy Spirit as the Messiah, the
   Christ.
. . .
We thank you, Father, for the water of baptism.
. . . we are buried with Christ
. . . we share in his resurrection
. . . we are reborn by the Holy Spirit.
. . .
Now sanctify this water that, by the power of your Holy Spirit,
they may be cleansed from sin . . . born again . . .
Renewed in your image . . .

from the Prayer over the Water

Using these biblical images gives us an opportunity to tell the Bible stories, often unknown or long-forgotten. Making the effort to explain the allusions will increase the meaning of the service for the families when the big day comes, for they will recognize the images as they occur in the prayer. Many of the visitors at baptisms have little knowledge of the Bible and it is clear that the imagery in the Prayer over the Water rings no bells for them, because they lose interest and begin to fidget. If we can begin to tell those stories to the families, then at least some of them will find something to latch on to.

A note regarding rehearsals

Godparents come from far and near and it is not usually possible to have them present at the preparation for baptism. If they can be there to walk and talk through the service on the previous day, that can be a tremendous asset. Not only does it avoid the need for a stream of stage directions during the service, it also helps them to practise saying their words clearly and audibly. If they don't have a practice with you, then they may well be sight-reading on the day. One godparent I know of hadn't had a look at the words before the service:

> 'Do you repent of the sins that separate us from God and neighbour?' asked the minister. 'I repeat them', came back the reply!

Children

There is much creative preparation that can be done with children who are old enough to understand, depending on their age. Bible stories can be acted out with familiar toys, videos watched, pictures painted, songs sung, water played with and so on. One approach is to explore some of the symbols and build on them, basing the preparation on activities surrounding the symbols and the words which accompany them.

So we might think about water while playing with it and connect our activity with some of the words quoted above, from the Prayer over the Water.

Or light:

> In baptism, God calls us out of darkness into his
> marvellous light.
>
> *Decision*
>
> *All* **Shine as a light in the world**
> **to the glory of God the Father.**
>
> *Giving of a Lighted Candle*

Or the oil of chrism:

> May God, who has received you by baptism into his Church,
> pour upon you the riches of his grace,
> that within the company of Christ's pilgrim people
> you may daily be renewed by his anointing Spirit,
> and come to the inheritance of the saints in glory. **Amen.**
>
> *Prayer after Baptism*

Here are some words which were originally put into the
Commission especially with older children in mind, and which
may now be used for any candidate:

> *N and N,*
> today God has touched you with his love
> and given you a place among his people.
> God promises to be with you
> in joy and in sorrow,
> to be your guide in life,
> and to bring you safely to heaven.
> In baptism God invites you on a life-long journey.
> Together with all God's people
> you must explore the way of Jesus
> and grow in friendship with God,
> in love for his people,
> and in serving others.
> With us you will listen to the word of God
> and receive the gifts of God.
>
> *from the Commission*

There are lots of ideas here that can be explored through games and stories. If, by the end of their preparation, the children are quite familiar with this particular text, it could be specially printed out to be kept inside a card or a Bible.

Adults

Anyone who has ministered to someone very ill and barely conscious will know how deeply moving it is when a familiar prayer sparks speech into life. People who have grown up regularly reciting the same prayers week in, week out, will have the rhythms and words so firmly etched in their memory that they become almost part of their being.

Similarly, people who have faced frightening and dark experiences have recounted how well-known prayers and Bible passages, ingrained in their memories from childhood, have kindled their faith and provided them with sustenance and encouragement from God.

However, because of a number of factors, Christians are decreasingly likely to memorize prayers and passages in this way today. What can be done about it?

A knapsack for the expedition

Helping candidates to memorize certain texts when they are preparing for baptism is one way in which we can equip them to cope with the ups and downs of life ahead. It has been suggested that the Church should encourage enquirers and followers to pack up a 'knapsack', or small collection, of essential prayers, psalms and other Bible passages to carry with them on the journey. Some of these might be central texts, shared by the whole Church, whilst others will be special to each individual. (Naturally, this could also be a helpful exercise for any Church member to do, however long they have been a Christian.)

Four texts in particular have been identified as core texts to include in the pack:

- The Lord's Prayer

- The Apostles' Creed

- The Beatitudes

- Jesus' summary of the Law

The first two of these are clearly part of every baptism service and the third is one of the suggested gospel readings at All Saints, so adult candidates for baptism are bound to come across them sooner or later. In the Early Church and in some traditions today the Church makes much more of them, however. Important texts are 'presented' to people who are preparing for baptism. The candidates are expected to learn them off by heart and the presentation is accompanied by a short form of service.

I am not proposing that we should test each candidate in advance of baptism in the middle of a Sunday service! We could do much more, though, to underline the value of these ancient texts in our baptism preparation by using them creatively and regularly, and by encouraging the candidates to memorize them for their own benefit. *Rites on the Way* contains short prayers and words which could appropriately be used with these core texts and enhance their significance. These could be adapted for use in a number of contexts: a baptism preparation group, a quiet mid-week service or even a main Sunday service. In this case, the high profile of initiation in the Church and the importance given to preparation of the candidates will challenge us and remind us all of our involvement in the process. It is much easier for a congregation to support the candidates in their final steps towards initiation if they are included and informed.

It is interesting to find out which other prayers and Bible verses are special to people. A baptism preparation group could swap ideas and help each other to fill their knapsacks with nourishing supplies. If candidates have little or no Christian background, we could suggest a few of our own favourites.

Further suggestions

Beyond the idea of a knapsack, many other sections of the service can be a valuable basis for creative study in preparation with a group or an individual. The suggestions in this chapter are by no means exhaustive, as we shall discover for ourselves as the services become increasingly familiar with use. Two other sections can form a good basis for fruitful discussion in the preparation of adults: the questions at the Decision (printed below) and the (adult) Commission (a précis of which is printed on page 33).

Do you reject the devil and all rebellion against God?
I reject them.

Do you renounce the deceit and corruption of evil?
I renounce them.

Do you repent of the sins that separate us from
   God and neighbour?
I repent of them.

Do you turn to Christ as Saviour?
I turn to Christ.

Do you submit to Christ as Lord?
I submit to Christ.

Do you come to Christ, the way, the truth and the life?
I come to Christ.

from the Decision

Both these sections open up opportunities to explore what the questions actually mean, and the implications of our replies to them. The wealth of the texts also presents us with openings to discuss all sorts of issues to do with God or our own discipleship. If there are a number of candidates being prepared, it is well worth taking time to discover the variety of answers that will emerge and engage in some lively interaction.

Words alone can be very dull and that is not a description we would want to use of our preparation meetings for baptism (or confirmation). But the words of the service can be used to good effect, bringing them alive as we connect them to our day to day experience, as we explore them through example and illustration and expand upon them by creative activity.

Preparing the congregation before the service

All the pastoral services in *Common Worship* have been given a 'Pastoral Introduction', a short piece of writing which can be read by the congregation before the service begins. It explains a bit about the service, and helps people to focus on and understand what will be taking place once the service begins. The services which come into the category of being 'pastoral' for this feature are: Baptism, Thanksgiving for the Gift of a Child, Marriage and Funeral.

There are often a great number of visitors at these services, many of whom are unfamiliar with the Church and have only hazy ideas of what to expect. The pastoral introductions are intended to give them a clearer picture, prepare the congregation for the service and help everyone to feel comfortable with what is happening. Having something to do once they sit down – reading the pastoral introduction – may also help visitors to settle in an environment that may seem strange and a little daunting.

But, of course, the introduction is not only for those who rarely set foot inside a church building; it will be just as interesting for regular members of the congregation, who will appreciate having their memories refreshed and their prayers guided.

The Pastoral Introduction to the baptism service begins by describing what baptism signifies in the life of the candidates. It sets the event within the context of the church community and gives the readers the opportunity to reflect upon their own baptism – if they have been baptized – and their progress on the journey. The Pastoral Introduction then highlights some of the symbolic imagery that is used in the service, giving simple explanations of its meaning, and inviting people to see the symbols as 'pictures', depicting what happens on the Christian way. Finally it suggests to the reader how he or she might pray for the candidates.

Pastoral Introductions can be found before the beginning of some of the key services in the main volume of *Common Worship* and the *Pastoral Services*. They can be printed in any locally produced order of service.

10 Where do we go from here?

The worldwide and extravagant celebrations on 31 December 1999 marked the end of an era for many people, old and young. It was the time to close the door on an old century and a past millennium, to learn by one's mistakes and look towards the future with a bright new hope, or so we were led to believe by all the hype. The date-line was crossed, the earth continued to turn and people carried on with their lives after a few days of holiday.

Without the clamour of such festivities, 31 December 2000 is the date marking the end of a different era, the end of twenty years' authorization of *The Alternative Service Book*. What are we to do in order to settle into using the *Common Worship* Initiation Services?

Parochial Church Councils

Canon B 3 covers the question of who decides which services are to be used in a parish when there is more than one authorized form available. The decision about Holy Communion, Morning and Evening Prayer and Services of the Word will be for the minister and the PCC to agree. The choice will be between *The Book of Common Prayer* and *Common Worship*. Before a church moves over from the ASB to *Common Worship*, therefore, the matter should be brought to the PCC so that it can be discussed and an agreement reached.

In most cases, the transfer from one set of modern language services to another will be a mere formality. It is unlikely that a church that has settled into worship in contemporary English will have any dispute concerning a transfer to *Common Worship*. The assumption that there need not be a discussion at all, however, would be bad practice and deny the PCC an ideal opportunity to pray and reflect upon the church's worship and mission. And while worship is on the agenda, it might also be a good time to review the parish's pattern of services.

Baptism

Approval of the PCC is *not* necessary, however, when it comes to choosing a form of baptism (or marriage, or funeral). This decision rests with the officiating minister on each occasion. If the minister chooses the *Common Worship* baptism and it is in the context of a *Common Worship* Holy Communion, for example, the decision is straightforward. Should the PCC resolve to use BCP services at some points, however, the minister will have to think very carefully: should she or he use the BCP baptism so that the language matches or can the *Common Worship* baptism be used with integrity?

The liturgical revision which produced the ASB resulted in a polarity between texts old and new. This time round the Liturgical Commission is encouraging us to make sensible use of both, alongside each other, rather as many churches already do with hymns and songs. It is difficult to dovetail a *Common Worship* baptism into a sung BCP evensong, although it can be done.

Confirmation

When it comes to confirmation, the decision rests with neither the PCC nor the parish priest but with the bishop.

Theology

Despite the fact that PCCs are not obliged to discuss which form of an occasional office is used, it is vitally important that the PCC is given the opportunity to grasp the developments in the Church's understanding of baptism. There has been much rediscovery over the past hundred years or so and a great deal of the thought and discussion has taken place between a relatively small minority of 'specialists', and it will take a while for this theology to filter through to the rest of the Church. Congregations do not absorb apparently revolutionary concepts instantaneously by osmosis! We need to give our PCCs the chance to understand what we have already discovered, which is reflected in the *Common Worship* Initiation Services. Then we shall have to plan a strategy for spreading the news to the pews!

Buildings and furniture

In earlier chapters of this book, much has been said about the way we use our church buildings: the spaces we create around important focal points and the positioning of these features; patterns of movement that we might make around different parts of the building; places for the congregation, the candidates and their supporters; and places for the president and other ministers. It is quite amazing the difference in atmosphere that can be created in a worship environment by rearranging the furniture (if it's moveable). Once the church has become excited by the theology of initiation, perhaps the people would like to share their ideas and set up a special task group to consider experimenting with the layout inside the building. Don't forget that, besides rearranging, we can also consider incorporating something new, or excluding a piece of furniture or an object that has outlived its usefulness. Our buildings are very often overloaded with an accumulation of inherited and ancient objects.

More radical reordering might also result from a PCC and community catching the vision of the transforming work of God in initiation. The possibilities of enhancing the church's celebrations could stimulate a fundamental reappraisal of the church's worship space.

Baptism policy

In Chapter 1 of this book, we recognized the challenge facing us as a church as we seek to baptize with integrity. We make some big promises to play our part in the nurture of the candidates, and we so often fail to keep them. We also recognize the gulf which lies between our own understanding of baptism and that of the many young families who bring their babies for the sacrament. If the PCC can reach a deeper appreciation of the issues involved, it may also want to reassess the parish baptism policy. We all need to take a long hard look at the systems in place for welcoming enquirers and guiding them forward in their search. We must also work to find ways of involving the whole church, at all stages of discipleship, in our programmes of nurture and growth, both before and after baptism, recognizing that for every one of us there will be times both of leading and of being led. And we have to look into the future, too, setting out patterns of nourishment that will enable the whole fellowship to grow in faith and knowledge of God.

A tough assignment? Indeed. But a wonderful – and imperative – task; baptism is one of the most exciting things that a church can do. And, at the end of the day, it is the heart of the Church's mission.

Pass it on

Jesus has the final word:

> Go and make disciples of all nations, baptizing them in the name of the Father and of the Son and of the Holy Spirit, and teaching them to obey everything that I have commanded you. And remember, I am with you always, to the end of the age.
>
> *Matthew 28.19,20*

Booklist and resources

Authorized and commended liturgical material

The Book of Common Prayer

Common Worship: Calendar, Lectionary and Collects, Church House Publishing, 1997.

Common Worship: Initiation Services, Church House Publishing, 1998.

Common Worship: Services and Prayers for the Church of England, Church House Publishing, 2000.
   Includes the latest form of A Service of the Word, Thanksgiving for the Gift of a Child and much of Holy Baptism.

Lent, Holy Week, Easter, Church House Publishing/Cambridge University Press/SPCK, 1984, 1986.
   A collection of seasonal resources, as the title suggests.

Patterns for Worship, Church House Publishing, 1995 (new edition due 2001/2).
   An essential tool, containing:

   - outline structure of A Service of the Word (as authorized in 1993);
   - a great deal of resource material for seasons and other themes, grouped under headings (e.g. confessions, absolutions, prayers, introductions to the Peace);
   - an extensive commentary explaining how to plan and prepare a Service of the Word.

The Promise of His Glory, Church House Publishing/Mowbray, 1991.
   A collection of resource material for the period from All Saints to Candlemas.

Electronic liturgy

Common Worship Visual Liturgy 3.0 (service and worship planning software), Church House Publishing, November 2000.
   A program containing authorized and commended liturgy, ideal for producing local orders of service (including baptism and confirmation), finding options and alternatives easily, making overhead projector acetates, or printing out specific prayers for congregational use.

Common Worship Text Disk, Church House Publishing, 2000.

Church of England web-site: *www.cofe.anglican.org*
   The *Common Worship* services can be downloaded from here.

Other liturgical material

Michael Perry, *The Dramatised Bible*, Marshal/Pickering, 1989.
   Using text straight from the New International Version and the Good News Bible, the whole Bible narrative has been dramatized for different voices. It is fun to use and puts vitality into our Bible readings. Ideal for all-age baptism services.

Rites on the Way: work in progress, a paper from the Liturgical Commission, GS misc 530, July 1998.
   A draft book of ideas for prayers and short forms of service which can be used in a variety of situations before and after baptism. There will be more to come but this is useful in the meantime.

Useful books

Mark Earey, *Producing Your Own Orders of Service*, Church House Publishing/*Praxis*, 2000.
   Immensely helpful to any church producing its own service cards or booklets. Down-to-earth, practical advice on every aspect from font size (printing, not baptismal!) and layout to

headings and pictures, offering clear liturgical principles behind the recommendations.

John Finney, *Finding Faith Today*, British and Foreign Bible Society, 1992.
Important and fascinating research into patterns of conversion, presented in a readable and accessible way.

Nick and Hazel Whitehead, *Baptism Matters*, National Society/ Church House Publishing, 1998.
Practical advice on using the *Common Worship* Baptism Service, including baptism preparation, how to choose godparents, outlines for all-age talks at baptism and baptism follow-up.

Background and theology

Colin Buchanan and Michael Vasey, *New Initiation Rites*, Grove Books, 1998.
All about the *Common Worship* Initiation Services: where they have come from, changes, and how to use them. And all in 28 pages.

J. G. Davies, *A New Dictionary of Liturgy and Worship*, SCM, 1986.
A book that you can dip into, covering any issue of Christian initiation you can think of (amongst many other things).

Martin Dudley and Geoffrey Rowell (eds), *The Oil of Gladness – Anointing in the Christian Tradition*, SPCK, 1993.
A collection of essays exploring the many different uses of oil in the Church, past and present.

Richard Giles, *Re-Pitching the Tent*, Canterbury Press, Norwich, 1997; second edition 1999.
An inspiring, challenging (and sometimes outrageous) study of church buildings and how we use them. Many thoughts about baptism, nurture and movement in services. Lots of ideas for reordering.

Regina Kuehn, *A Place for Baptism*, Liturgy Training Publications, Chicago, 1992.

On the Way: Towards an Integrated Approach to Christian Initiation, Church House Publishing, 1995.
> The General Synod report which lays out the thinking behind the *Common Worship* Initiation Services. If you didn't think that reports could be exciting, try this one.

S. Anita Stauffer, *On Baptismal Fonts: Ancient and Modern*, Alcuin Club/GROW Liturgical Study 29–30, Grove Books, 1994.

Kenneth Stevenson, *The First Rites*, Lamp Press, 1989.
> Exploring all aspects of worship in the Early Church.

E. C. Whitaker, *Documents of the Baptismal Liturgy*, SPCK, 1970.
> This is the book to look at if you actually want to see the texts that have been used for baptism through the centuries.

E. C. Whitaker, *The Baptismal Liturgy*, SPCK, 1981.
> A concise historical look at baptism through the ages.

Notes

Chapter 2: Symbols

1. Stephen Platten, 'The Bible, symbolism and liturgy', in Kenneth W. Stevenson (ed.), *Symbolism and the Liturgy II*, Grove Books, 1981.
2. E. C. Whitaker, *The Baptismal Liturgy*, SPCK, 1981, p. 35.
3. John Chrysostom, *Baptismal Homilies* 2.24, cited in E. C. Yarnold, *The Awe-Inspiring Rites of Initiation: Baptismal Homilies of the Fourth Century*, St Paul Publications, 1972.

Chapter 3: Enhancing the imagery

1. Richard Giles, *Re-Pitching the Tent*, Canterbury Press, 1997; 2nd edn, 1999.

Chapter 5: Which service do we use?

1. *Praxis*/Church House Publishing, 2000.
2. Michael Perry, *The Dramatised Bible*, Marshall Pickering, 1989.

Index